BLACK LIVES AND SACRED HUMANITY

Black Lives and Sacred Humanity

Toward an African American Religious Naturalism

Carol Wayne White

FORDHAM UNIVERSITY PRESS

New York 2016

Fordham University Press gratefully acknowledges
financial assistance provided for the publication of
this book from the Offices of the Provost and the
Dean of Arts & Sciences, Bucknell University.

Copyright © 2016 Fordham University Press

Fordham University Press has no responsibility for the
persistence or accuracy of URLs for external or third-party
Internet websites referred to in this publication and does
not guarantee that any content on such websites is, or will
remain, accurate or appropriate.

Fordham University Press also publishes its books in a
variety of electronic formats. Some content that appears in
print may not be available in electronic books.
Visit us online at www.fordhampress.com.

Library of Congress Cataloging-in-Publication Data
Names: White, Carol Wayne, (date)– author.
Title: Black lives and sacred humanity : toward an African
American religious naturalism / Carol Wayne White.
Description: New York : Fordham University Press,
[2016] | Includes bibliographical references and index. |
Description based on print version record and CIP data
provided by publisher; resource not viewed.
Identifiers: LCCN 2016005571 (print) | LCCN 2015042062
(ebook) | ISBN 9780823269839 (ePub) |
ISBN 9780823269815 (cloth : alk. paper) |
ISBN 9780823269822 (pbk. : alk. paper)
Subjects: LCSH: African Americans—Religion.
Classification: LCC BL2525 (print) | LCC BL2525
.W473 2016 (ebook) | DDC 200.89/96073—dc23
LC record available at http://lccn.loc.gov/2016005571

Printed in the United States of America
18 17 16   5 4 3 2 1
First edition

CONTENTS

This study arises out of my ongoing interest in the creative interface of religion and science, or, more specifically, in current strains of religious naturalism. At Bucknell University, colleagues and students alike have experienced my enthusiasm for religious naturalism's emergence within the larger field of religious studies. In various academic settings beyond Bucknell, I have also shared my convictions about the pivotal role religious naturalism can play in helping humanistic scholars challenge outdated conceptions of a distinctive human nature in the West.

As an avid proponent of religious naturalism, I have been struck by the potential of its key ideas to address in innovative ways some major themes or concerns of African American religious thought, such as the effects of racist discourse on influential conceptions of our humanity. Sadly, many influential religious naturalism writings have not actively pursued this line of thought. (In a similar vein, as a philosopher of religion, I have found that major themes and contributions from black religious scholarship are seldom represented in the subfield of philosophy of religion.) Additionally, a survey of African American religious scholarship reveals a predominance of historical, theological, social-political, and cultural analyses that often ignore many of the epistemological and philosophical orientations that I find appealing within religious naturalism and critical theory or philosophy of religion. *Black Lives and Sacred Humanity* thus represents my desire to bring these fields of knowledge together as I focus on the conceptual, epistemological, and axiological import of a recurrent theme within black religiosity: the necessity of establishing and valuing blacks' humanity. In doing so, I aim to describe the emergence of an African American religious naturalism.

In a much wider theoretical context, the book addresses unexamined philosophical and humanistic assumptions embedded in contemporary African American religiosity. As an alternative to theistic models of African American religiosity and spirituality, this study is an unabashed celebration of religious humanism. I am hoping that its perspectives and main argument will inspire a generation of scientifically oriented African Americans in search of newer, conceptually compelling views of religiosity that address a classic, perennial religious question: What does it mean to be fully human and fully alive? The notion of sacred humanity I explore also provides a powerful new discursive context in which all contemporary readers, not just those of African descent, may grasp the ethical, axiological, and symbolic efficacy of African American religiosity in the contemporary scientific age.

In various disciplines, scholars of African American thought and culture are looking back to influential figures and retrieving their ideas to help us all think about and address the difficult legacy of racism that all of us have inherited, regardless of how we mark our identities. The book contributes to this trend in tracing the nuanced and fuller meanings of the sacred humanity concept in three iconic figures, Ann Julia Cooper, W. E. B. Du Bois, and James Baldwin, whose ideas are very influential today and receiving a renaissance of interest. Linking and reading Cooper, Du Bois, and Baldwin in this manner offers another level of appreciation for their genius; it also offers another way of thinking about and reading them in the larger context of American letters.

Finally, it is my hope that *Black Lives and Sacred Humanity* can contribute in some small way to ongoing, difficult conversations that seek to address the poignant and widening cultural divides surrounding race in North America today. Among other things, this book seeks to redirect our attention to a perceived (and for me, fundamental) truth that the construction of race obfuscates and distorts: the affirmation of our common, entangled humanity. As Cooper, Du Bois, and Baldwin all recognized before our generation, claiming this truth is essential to our national well-being. I believe, as they did, that what is at stake is the type of future we can create, or the type of transformed America we can become. At this critical juncture in our history, I believe one crucial task—and, for me, a quintessentially religious one—toward this goal is appreciating and embracing our *sacred* humanity and acting in accordance with this conviction.

BLACK LIVES AND SACRED HUMANITY

Introduction: In Search of a New Religious Ideal

In his groundbreaking volume *The Souls of Black Folk* (1903), W. E. B. Du Bois featured a lengthy essay, "Of the Faith of the Fathers," which revealed the distinctive character of African American culture during a critical time when the majority of black voices were muted or silenced. In the piece, Du Bois addresses the historical significance and remarkable resilience of African American religiosity as well as its major limitations. Synthesizing empirical data and theoretical insights, he offers a compelling vision of the complex unfolding of nineteenth-century African American religiosity—from its inception as slave religion to its distinct configurations in the North and South since emancipation. In sketching this evolution, Du Bois brings to light the institutionalization of a people's hopes, fears, core values, aspirations, ethical convictions, cosmological assumptions, and grasp of death. A notable feature of black religiosity captured by Du Bois is its emphasis on achieving radical transformations within North American culture, as seen in the final lines of the essay, which come directly after Du Bois's critical judgments of black culture and its inherent ethical (and religious) paradoxes:

But back of this still broods silently the deep religious feeling of the real Negro heart, the stirring, unguided might of powerful human souls who have lost the guiding star of the past and seek in the great night a new religious ideal. Some day the Awakening will come, when the pent-up vigor of ten million souls shall sweep irresistibly toward the Goal, out of the Valley of the Shadow of Death, where all that makes life worth living—Liberty, Justice, and Right—is marked "For White People Only."[1]

As this passage suggests, for Du Bois, studying the religious life of African Americans was a crucial task in presenting the inventiveness of a people who constantly struggled to inhabit their humanity and eke out a meaningful existence for themselves amid harrowing circumstances. Both here and elsewhere, Du Bois portrays African American religiosity fundamentally as an evolving humanistic enterprise with monumental social and communal implications.[2]

A century later, I find Du Bois's insights into African American religiosity compelling and just as relevant as they were in 1903. His provocative evocation of a new religious ideal emerging from past convictions is intriguing, inviting further scrutiny. Discerning an important intellectual task in the conceptual space opened by Du Bois, I consider anew the evolving nature of African American religiosity and its import in the contemporary era. In contemplating this task, I am confronted by several questions: What might constitute a new African American religious ideal in the twenty-first century? How might one see it emerging from past convictions? Is it possible to grasp a fuller sense of the rich, layered texture of African American religiosity with this new principle? In addressing these questions in this book, I explore a naturalistic framework for grasping the evolving nature of African American religiosity today.

Notwithstanding its range of theological expressions, African American religiosity overall has been vigilant in promoting a major theme of liberation since its inception and evolution from the historical experience of slavery. Specifically, this theme of liberation has been intimately and irretrievably connected to the necessity of affirming blacks' full humanity amid culturally coded racist rhetoric and practices. Consequently, I contend that African American religiosity has revealed a general structure of human desire that underscores the value of life, insisting on U.S. blacks' efforts to bring forth conditions that would promote the fullness of life for all those interested in processes of transformation. *Black Lives and Sacred Humanity* develops this theme, arguing for a radical humanism that claims a religious sensibility for itself. Identifying African American religiosity as blacks' ingenuity in relentlessly endeavoring to claim their full humanity and create a meaningful, dignified existence for themselves, I construct a concept of sacred humanity and ground it in iconic African American writings. More specifically, within the context of African American culture and history, I explore the notion of humans as interconnected, social, value-laden organisms in constant search of meaning (cognition), enamored of value (beauty, goodness, love), and instilled with a sense of purpose (telos). I deem this conception of humanity sacred in light of a naturalistic vision that emphasizes deep interconnectedness among human animals and our kinship with other sentient life forms, accentuating a modality of existence in which transformation occurs. With the concept of sacred humanity, I continue to affirm the vigor of African American religiosity in its fundamental propensity toward life. I also underscore the functional value of black religion as one of the highest aspirations of African American character: its claim on life.

The particular approach I use in establishing the notion of sacred humanity moves us beyond the metaphysical claims and conceptual idealism that often ground the dominant values discourse in traditional African American religiosity. Instead of locating African American valuing within the sphere of a transcendental deity, I look to newer insights emerging from religious naturalism that posit humans as evolving organisms inherently constituted by a particular matrix of values.[3] The rationale I provide for this concept of sacred humanity is compatible with the best of current scientific thought regarding deep relationality in biology and cosmology. Insights offered by neurologists and other scientists who emphasize the social character of cognition in human organisms and other animals also provide various types of evidence for understanding human beings as symbol makers, creators of a world imbued with value, and as social organisms. These resources help me avoid epistemological reductionism while acknowledging the complexity of material life, as evidenced by the human potential to envision and experience possibilities from within our current realities.[4]

After conceptualizing this notion of sacred humanity, I contend that it has been foreshadowed, very subtly and most intriguingly, in specific African American voices, perspectives, and cultural settings. Specifically, I trace indications of this concept in an intellectual-activist trajectory constituted by Anna Julia Cooper, W. E. B. Du Bois, and James Baldwin. Within this trajectory, one finds each figure offering systematic cognitive and ethical reflections on an expanded model of humanity that goes beyond those that were operative within the racial discourses of their respective eras. Granted, Cooper, Du Bois, and Baldwin are not the only black voices to reject problematic racial categories pertaining to the humanity of blacks, as there is innumerable wealth and a wide range of unexplored figures in African American intellectual thought. However, Cooper, Du Bois, and Baldwin are important to this study because they dared to embrace alternative value systems and cosmological perspectives outside of traditional religious thought as they challenged the state of affairs affecting their black contemporaries. In the process, these visionary intellectuals imagined (or conceived) what humanity could be, beyond what was experienced or envisioned at the beginning of and well into the twentieth century. While historically they cannot be read as religious naturalists *per se*, they certainly foreshadow key ideas that I advance as a contemporary religious naturalist. The link between their historic insurrections and the ideas I explore in this study constitutes the enduring legacy of those who have dared to dream of a better America. In the final chapter of this work, I suggest that this linkage provides the inception of a new religious ideal, or the emergence of religious naturalism, within African American culture.

Offering an alternative to theistic assumptions about African American religiosity and spirituality, *Black Lives and Sacred Humanity* provides a fuller sense of the rich and layered texture of African American religiosity in the contemporary era. This book is an unabashed celebration of religious humanism, and I believe its major ideas have the potential to inspire a generation of scientifically oriented African Americans in search of newer, conceptually compelling views of religiosity that address a classic, perennial question: What does it mean to be fully human and fully alive? The notion of sacred humanity I explore also provides a powerful new discursive context within which all contemporary readers, not just those of African descent, can grasp the ethical, axiological, and symbolic efficacy of African American religiosity in the contemporary scientific age.

In developing this concept of sacred humanity, I share the conviction among contemporary religious scholars that the complexity of beliefs, choices, and actions of Africans Americans are not reducible to traditional expressions of black religion, or to the black church tradition—an important idea that came to the fore in Charles Long's important work *Significations: Signs, Symbols, and Images in the Interpretation of Religion* (1999).[5] My interests thus coincide with those of scholars who see the necessity of addressing the wider set of discourses and ideas associated with African American values, expressions, and movements aimed at liberation and transformation. With them, I prefer to address the contours of African

American religiosity within a larger context of humanistic scholarship, thereby contributing to various attempts to rethink the canon from which religious scholars and theologians draw. Specifically, the methodological orientation I explore overlaps with those of Victor Anderson, Cornel West, and Anthony Pinn, who have provided compelling philosophical analyses or general cultural/theoretical examinations of African American religiosity, offering in their respective works such provocative notions as "ontological blackness," "radical democracy," and "African American humanism." [6] Pinn, in particular, has produced two works that reflect, in part, the conceptual space in which I explore. In *Terror and Triumph* (2003), he argues that at its core African American religion is a quest for subjectivity, and he analyzes African American religion from the perspective of its existential and ontological concerns. Pinn continues exploring his alternative theory of African American religion in *What Is African American Religion?* (2011), focusing on the notion of a pervasive, "embodied" elemental impulse that symbolizes humanity's desire for transformation and its quest for meaning.[7] *Black Lives and Sacred Humanity* shares the general perspective that black religiosity has focused on liberating blacks from unsavory and questionable views of our humanity. Perhaps my extensive use of and direct appeal to religious naturalism as my theoretical framework will make evident my focus on constructing a theory of the human within the tenets of that framework, rather than assuming its meaning.

Furthermore, in grounding this model of religiosity in religious naturalism, I share the concerns of the many religious scholars invested in keeping our discipline relevant within an increasingly complex intellectual milieu. As suggested by Russell McCutcheon's provocative study *The Discipline of Religion: Structure, Meaning, Rhetoric* (2003), asking about religion's purview in a contemporary context of increasing philosophical and sociological sophistication has become a crucial and ongoing concern for religious scholars.[8] I am invigorated and compelled by the potential value of religious naturalism in this context, as I think it offers another epistemological and methodological possibility for addressing the crucial issue of religion's influence today and indicating the unique value of religious studies in the contemporary university.

Black Lives and Sacred Humanity is divided into two major sections, and the first two chapters lay much of the conceptual ground for later explorations. Chapter 1 offers the first of two major theoretical discussions in which I begin constructing the sacred humanity concept. I argue that the concept emerges from a creative synthesis of African American religious-intellectual thought and critical theory, showing how each of these discourses provides important insights that make possible the coherency and intelligibility of the term. Here, the theoretical richness embedded in the cultural exigencies of African Americans having to justify and humanize their existence also comes into play.

In chapter 2, I continue establishing the theoretical framework for my conception of sacred humanity. I introduce scientific theories advanced by religious naturalism that help me to envision humanity as a specific life form, or as nature made aware of itself. I also define human beings as sacred centers of value and distinct movements of nature itself, in which deep relationality and interconnectedness become key metaphors for understanding what constitutes our processes of becoming human. Finally, I set this view of humanity within the context of African American culture and history to underscore the conceptual richness of the liberationist motif within black religiosity and to celebrate its enduring legacy. With the concept of sacred humanity, I thus bring to light newer, deeper understandings of key basic convictions in African American religious expression.

Chapters 3, 4, and 5 then trace the subtle presence of the new religious ideal of sacred humanity within the writings of Cooper, Du Bois, and Baldwin, underscoring the ways in which their critical analyses and expanded views of humanity contribute to an African American religious naturalism. In chapter 3, I introduce Anna Julia Cooper's late-nineteenth-century romanticized feminism, discussing her creative use of nature as a trope for inspiring the young American nation to rid itself of its racist and sexist practices and become an arena in which all human beings can flourish. I also discuss the theoretical underpinnings of Cooper's expanded view of humanity, showing her points of convergence with Goethe's philosophy of science and her vision of a communal ontology that is often a key idea within later developments in religious naturalism. Finally, I argue that Cooper's Romantic vision anticipates the capacious humanistic view I develop with the concept of sacred humanity. In this respect, her ideas provide a nice entry point to the African American intellectual trajectory that I see contributing to the emergence of my African American religious naturalism.

Chapter 4 explores the subtleties and layers of meaning in W. E. B. Du Bois's early-twentieth-century emphasis on human ingenuity within the African American religious context, emphasizing his view of religion as a natural process generated by the finite conditions of human life, or under the specter of raced living. These intriguing aspects of his anti-transcendental approaches to black religiosity dovetail with my theoretical convictions, and I further examine the resonances between Du Bois's

forward-thinking views of black humanity and my concept of human destinies as precious centers of value. As in the case of Cooper, so in select
writings of Du Bois I discern an expanded model of humanity that reaches
beyond those that dominated the racial discourses of the writer's era.

In chapter 5, I focus on James Baldwin's efforts during the mid–
twentieth century to enhance race relations in the United States with an
expanded view of humanity and our capacity to love one another. I introduce Baldwin's critical perspectives that conjoined religion and race. Of
importance here are Baldwin's warnings against investing in a religious
vision that implicitly kept in place white racist constructs and problematic cultural practices. With an eye toward expanding his contemporaries'
views of their constitutive humanity, Baldwin emphasized embodied forms
of love that he believed would result in the vital flourishing of all North
Americans. This chapter associates Baldwin's contribution to the sacred
humanity concept with his critical sense of black human beings as lovers of
life at a critical juncture in American history.

The conclusion ties together the various themes found in Cooper,
Du Bois, and Baldwin with my conceptual concerns, showing the emergence of an African American religious naturalism. I offer brief reflections
on the major motifs developed throughout the various chapters. Specifically, I summarize key aspects of my sacred humanity model of African
American religious naturalism, highlight important implications, and offer
a sense of its potential value in African American life and in the nation
at large.

CHAPTER I

African American Religious Sensibilities and the Question of the Human

We are unknown, we knowers, ourselves to ourselves: this has its
own good reason. We have never searched for ourselves—how
should it then come to pass, that we should ever *find* ourselves?

—FRIEDRICH NIETZSCHE

The notion of sacred humanity I explore emerges from a creative synthesis
of African American religious and intellectual thought, critical theory, and
religious naturalism. Each of these discourses provides important insights
that make possible the coherency and intelligibility of the term. I focus
on the first two in this chapter, later addressing religious naturalism in
chapter 2. To begin my argument, I first provide historical examples of
the enduring legacy of African American religiosity as it emerged from the
wreckages of slavery, underscoring it as one distinct and critical response
by blacks attempting to defy dehumanizing practices and racist rhetoric
in the United States. I specifically identify a thematic pattern within black
religious thought that illustrates the various ways African Americans have
sought to humanize their existence and flourish as a people.[1] With these
examples, I underscore the functional value of black religiosity and dis-
tinguish this humanistic bent as one of the highest aspirations of African
American character, namely, its claim on life.

I then set this functionalist approach to black religiosity within a wider
conceptual context that renders a sense of its richness and value: a modern
Euro-American philosophical trajectory that has shifted attention away

from the traditional object of faith (deity) to emphasize human subjectivity. As I suggest, this modernist shift, of which the Enlightenment is a paradigmatic example, failed to live up to its emancipatory aims, ushering in an influential cultural ethos with deficient models of humanity supported by influential forms of racialized reasoning. Key for my purposes are the creative responses from black intellectual culture in the mid–twentieth century in addressing the lethal effects of this "enlightened" humanistic discourse. These critical perspectives provide the backdrop for my development of a new African American religious ideal emerging out of old convictions; in short, these responses help give shape to the view of sacred humanity that I begin constructing in chapter 2.

African American Religious Valuing

In the significant study *African American Religious Thought: An Anthology* (2003), Cornel West and Eddie S. Glaude, Jr. divided the evolution of African American religious life into five critical phases: 1) African American religion as the problem of slavery (mid–eighteenth century to 1863); 2) African American religion and the problem(s) of emancipation (1864– 1903); 3) African American religion, the city, and the challenge to racism (1903–1954); 4) African American religion and the black freedom struggle (1954–1969); 5) the golden age of African American religious studies (1969–present).[2]

A cursory look at this typology shows African American religiosity evolving historically (and perhaps primarily) as a complex socioethical, political mechanism that has aided African Americans in their myriad struggles against various forms of injustice—a key point expressed by Du Bois in *The Souls of Black Folk*.

This evolution is not surprising, given the harrowing experiences of Africans on this continent as enslaved subjects whose full humanity was often questioned or denied.[3] Once transported onto American shores, the physical color of Africans took on symbolic significance within a cultural system of differentiation that both marked them as slaves and justified negative assessments of their humanity. With the establishment of slave laws during the colonial period, whites were justified in treating blacks as objects or assets to be bought and sold, mortgaged and wagered, devised and condemned. In very few contexts were blacks regarded as human subjects with volition, feeling, and a sense of responsibility. Their slave status stripped them of many civil rights and liberties purportedly granted to all citizens of the nation, such as the right to make contracts or other legally binding choices, to sue or be sued, to acquire property, to marry legally, and (with rare exceptions) to testify against whites.[4] Along with other cultural practices, these laws were integral to a white supremacist ideology that systemically devalued black lives and attempted to place blacks outside of the circle of full humanity. Historical records show that this ideological apparatus in the United States has been very hard to dismantle. (In the contemporary era, the development of Critical Race Theory has emerged from legal scholars' awareness of the power structures based on white privilege and white supremacy that have continued to perpetuate the marginalization of all people of color.[5]) During the processes of securing legal, social, and political gains in subsequent centuries, people of African descent have continually encountered views of themselves as inferior, as subhuman beasts, outsiders, even as interlopers—even up to the present era.[6]

Religious expression has been one of the key strategies used by African Americans attempting to free themselves from these conceptions and the problematic cultural practices ensuing from them. While an exhaustive treatise on the complex evolution of black religiosity in this regard falls beyond the scope of this study, there are key moments and a discernible pattern through the years that can be identified. Emerging as it did from the context of slavery, the dominant African American cultural narrative is replete with religious interventions and strategies that provided the necessary ontological justification and ethical reasoning for establishing blacks' full humanity. For example, the use of spirituals in slave religion represents one of the earliest recorded acts of resistance against an institution that defined blacks fundamentally as property. With these ancient songs, slaves (individually and communally) attempted some measure of freedom in acknowledging a divine presence that affirmed their humanity in ways dominant white culture did not.[7]

In the process of trying to comprehend the wretched processes of slavery, literate African Americans with rich theological imaginations also employed various forms of biblical hermeneutics directed toward their full emancipation. Varied abolitionists and reformers in the nineteenth century often referenced the Exodus narrative of the ancient Hebrews as a key metaphor for their own sociopolitical activism.[8] The exodus event served a broader agenda of assisting influential leaders as they developed a concept of national identity that reflected the black slaves' unique experience; inspired by the epic narrative of Moses and the Israelites, many blacks looked beyond their oppressed status to a future when they would be authentically free, exercising their rights as complex human beings. Nineteenth-century religious thinkers and visionaries such as Isabella Baumfree (known as Sojourner Truth) and Alexander Crummell reminded the young nation that a fundamental distortion of the value of all human life was operative in the nation's failure to establish and maintain the proper material conditions and social conventions that would enable African Americans to flourish individually and collectively.[9] Together with other iconic figures, they consistently decried the dehumanizing factors embedded in America's social and legal institutions while addressing the existential and psychological factors that contributed to African Americans' sense of selfhood and assertions of their humanity.

The use of transcendental theological language was indispensable for many leaders who inspired their communities with a vision of freedom. For example, Maria W. Miller Stewart, a social activist and public speaker during the early nineteenth century, believed her activism was a dimension of divine justice operating in the world—a theme that has consistently resurfaced in subsequent African American religious perspectives. In her speeches and rhetorical gestures as an abolitionist speaking on behalf of the African American Female Intelligence Society of Boston, Stewart appealed to a divine agency—or what she described as the divine "Word" as written in the world through the deeds and actions of the faithful.[10] In Stewart's paradigmatic case, the notion of divine justice provided the quintessential ethical standard for addressing the dehumanizing structures of American culture, and it served to adjudicate internal conflicts (for example, sexism) within black culture. When one of the more influential abolitionist newspapers counseled that "the voice of woman should not be heard in public debates, but there are other ways in which her influences would be beneficial,"[11] Stewart bravely declared:

> What if I am a woman; is not the God of ancient times the God of these modern days? Did he not raise up Deborah, to be a mother, and a judge in Israel? Did not Queen Esther save the lives of the Jews? And Mary Magdalene first declare the resurrection of Christ from the dead? . . . If such women as are here described have once existed, be no longer astonished then, my brethren and friends, that God at this eventful period should raise up your own females to strive, by their example, both in public and private, to assist those who are endeavoring to stop the current of prejudice that flows so profusely against us at present.[12]

Stewart's speeches and activism constituted a critical (albeit early) phase of a distinct cultural trajectory that established an important set of values aimed at dignifying blacks' humanity and enriching the lives of all, not just a select few.

As the most influential African American religious tradition of that period, Christianity inspired countless blacks in their quests to negate the negation of their precious humanity within exploitative cultural systems.[13] In his classic study *The Negro Church in America*, E. Franklin Frazier described "black" Christianity as "a nation within a nation, espousing racial solidarity for black communities," and he highlighted the functional role of its symbols among African Americans in establishing their essential value as humans.[14] As these and other historical accounts show, many of the newly freed blacks who were introduced to Protestant Christianity saw within its symbolic language and eschatological visions an avenue toward liberation and transformation of self and society on multiple levels. One of the most enduring ideas operative in traditional black Christianity is the biblically inspired view of a personal deity (God) who acts in human history on behalf of the downtrodden and marginalized. The conceptual fullness and complexity of this theological notion within the long history of African American religious culture is impossible to sketch here; suffice it to say that the term *God* has been directly associated with immanent qualities of goodness, love, mercy, and justice in conjunction with idealized exercises of power and objective knowledge.

In his 1938 study *The Negro's God*, Benjamin Mays examined some of the earliest conceptions of God in African American literature written in distinct periods: 1760–1865; the Civil War period to 1914; and 1914–1937.[15] According to Mays, from 1760 to 1914 the idea of God developed along two main trajectories: 1) views of God that were used to support or encourage adherence to traditional, compensatory patterns that addressed earthly sufferings; and 2) conceptions of God, whether traditional or otherwise, that were developed and interpreted to support a growing consciousness of social and psychological adjustment needed in the quest for freedom. The sentiments of an anonymous ex-slave appear to illustrate this latter point, as his musings on the concept of God are inextricably tied to his sense of being a reflective, ensouled human: "There is a man in a man. The soul is the medium between God and man. God speaks to us through our conscience, and the reasoning is so loud that we seem to hear a voice."[16] Notwithstanding the shifts in emphasis indicated by these two lines of thought, Mays acknowledges that formative theistic affirmations among African Americans were always firmly situated in the social situation of the people.

Following Mays' lead in this regard is James Evans, a contemporary theologian, who has recently argued that historically the experience of otherness constituting the lived experiences of black Americans has been inextricably connected to particular conceptions of God. Evans states: "In situations where their humanity is called into question in subtle and not so subtle ways, African Americans cannot talk about God without talking about what it means to be black in the United States. In situations where African Americans affirm their humanity in spite of their dehumanization they cannot talk about what it means to be black without talking about God as the arbiter of human worth."[17] These examples from Mays and Evans help to illustrate, among other things, an important point in grasping the functional value of traditional black religiosity: theistic affirmations have been closely associated with a fundamental epistemic assertion that has, by necessity, been established repeatedly in every generation, that is, the assertion that all humans share in the same ontological reality.[18] This truth claim often propels the myriad forms of social and political activism in black culture that have continually challenged our various institutions to enact that principle in earnest.

In the mid–twentieth century, black religious expression took on distinct sociopolitical characteristics as many leaders continued the crucial task of countering racial discrimination and affirming the intrinsic value of black humanity. A key figure in this period was James Cone, whose articulation of a black liberation theology became a standard measure for adopting religious and ethical mandates against white racism. The liberationist paradigm that Cone helped to inaugurate has continued to reinforce black subjectivity as an ontological necessity as it has sought to achieve cultural integrity and wholeness in a race-driven culture.[19] Variations of this black theological consciousness have culminated in an influential corpus of African American religious thought and expression up to the present day. Furthermore, in recent decades, scholars have continued exploring the axiological, cultural, and social implications of this liberationist theme in exciting, bold directions, underscoring a black religiosity that addresses the prevalence and pernicious effects of institutionalized racism in the daily lives of African Americans.[20] Notable among these new perspectives are womanist religious expressions that have foregrounded black women's lived experience as a crucial starting point for sustained religious reflection on cultural survival and wholeness. As expressed by many of its proponents, womanist religious thought has emerged as a strategic intervention that focuses primarily on two destructive structures affecting the entire black community: white supremacy that denies full humanity to blacks, and patriarchal systems that obfuscate black women's humanity. As the pioneering work of Delores Williams indicates, womanist religious thought often evokes a cultural agenda bent on maintaining the integrity of black humanity through a shared struggle with varied marginalized black identities in the ongoing quest to survive and ensure a productive quality of life for all blacks in the United States.[21] Along with other contemporary initiatives, womanist reflections show that religious expression remains at the heart of African Americans' recorded quest for fullness of life in a nation that has often failed to fulfill—and often sadly, compromised on—its duty to secure the highest quality of life for all its denizens.

This thumbnail sketch of an evolving African American religiosity could never capture its full complexity, diversity, and richness; nonetheless, it serves to illuminate a recurrent liberationist theme that was born out of the historical realities of the slave experience and its aftermath. While acknowledging other possible interpretations, I believe this thematic pattern of liberation highlights African Americans' desire to live fully and with dignity. It also expresses a propensity toward life that is inextricably connected to affirming and establishing blacks' full humanity in a vexed, race-driven cultural context that has generated dehumanizing forces and structures on many levels. These observations support my view of black religiosity as a people's ongoing desire to achieve self-preservation, self-definition, and self-determination; it is, arguably, one of black culture's most vital productions. In making these claims, I am viewing African American religiosity primarily through the lens of religious functionalism, which, as Loyal Rue has suggested, places the proper focus on who actually creates and uses religion: humans.[22] Religious functionalism in this context is a method of analyzing and interpreting religious experiences and expressions as natural events having natural causes. This naturalistic approach seeks to understand religious phenomena by using categories, concepts, principles, and methods compatible with the ones normally applied to nonreligious domains of human behavior. In advancing this theoretical orientation, I do not presume that religious phenomena can be completely explained; rather, I suggest that the extent of our understanding is contingent on efforts to grasp these phenomena in terms of underlying natural processes.

In the Western history of ideas, this general approach is not new, having been advanced many times in the past. As Rue asserts, notable thinkers such as Kant, Feuerbach, Marx, Durkheim, and Freud have argued that "regardless of what religion *says* it is about, it has to *do* fundamentally with meeting the challenges to a full life."[23] I share with these earlier figures and with contemporary naturalists like Rue the conviction that religion both originates in human experience and is properly understood in natural terms, in contrast to those theories that see it emerging from some transcendent order or given by divine revelation. In this work, however, I offer a fresh iteration of this general humanistic orientation in setting it within the context of raced living in the United States. Briefly stated, my naturalistic approach examines the theme of liberation endemic to black religiosity in order to feature the ways African Americans have humanized their existence. Doing so, I believe, will bring renewed focus on blacks as complex humans expressing and experiencing religious truth claims, and will bring to light an important conceptual task: asking what it means to be human. This naturalistic turn is in keeping with recent developments in black religious scholarship that have advocated for a broader understanding of African American sources, norms, and teachings beyond traditional Christianity.[24]

As with other theoretical innovations in the larger field of religious studies, naturalism is not without its critics, many of whom have suggested that in modernity it has led inexorably to *secularization*. Within the context of black theological studies, for example, Vincent Lloyd's cautionary statement regarding black secularism comes to mind. For Lloyd and others sharing his perspective, the relatively new "secular age" carries with it some key assumptions about theological thinking that have led to theology's autonomy being lost and compromised. As he notes,

> Secularism is a dogmatic commitment to exclude the theological. . . . The theological and not the religious: there are many who diagnose intellectual problems with secularism and prescribe making room for religious reasons, or religious language, or religious practices. The academic humanities have seen much of this recently: a realization in history, anthropology, literature, and cultural studies that the religious has been excluded without reason, and must now be attended to. But secularism as I mean it is the foreclosure of the theological imagination, of that blend of beliefs, languages, and practices that acknowledges a religious "cultural-linguistic system"—or rather its theological doppelganger—not as an object of study but as that in which we participate, wittingly or unwittingly.[25]

Lloyd's concern for the eclipse of participatory theological truths pertaining to black culture remains important for those grasping the deep significance of institutionalized black religiosity, or even those interested in emphasizing the black church's role in valuing black identities and bodies in North America. However, as I seek to demonstrate, there is another way of interpreting the evolving vitality and beauty of black religious expression. When set within a naturalistic framework, black religiosity can also be examined and appreciated as an expression of the remarkable ingenuity of black humans seeking to dignify our existence—otherwise stated, it reflects a noble aspiration of black culture in making a claim on life. This approach, I believe, is consistent with its historical evolution and is reflective of the theme of liberation I have outlined.

The naturalistic approach I endorse in this study does not pretend to forge any intrinsic affinity with black theologians or religious scholars who continue to emphasize the uniqueness of black theological language and the confessional experiences of the black church in the lives of African Americans. In short, the thoroughgoing naturalism I espouse does not seek, in the last analysis, to justify black religion's epistemic claims with belief in a transcendent order of entities and events having causal influence on the order of nature. Operating on the assumption that the natural order is ultimately real, I am much more concerned about the human in its most concrete, basic terms: as a material process of nature in relationship with other forms of nature. Accordingly, I see markers of race, gender, class, sexuality, and so forth as cultural categories derived from this more fundamental complex nexus of materiality. Moreover, the naturalism I espouse here is not to be conflated with what Charles Taylor describes as an exclusive humanism that puts humans at the center of the universe.[26] Rather, with the tenets of religious naturalism that I flesh out in the next chapter, I view humans as a biotic form within a complex matrix of interdependent natural entities. Attempting a thoroughgoing naturalism that can also be equated with a meaningful or good life, I also view this fundamental kinship as sacred.

Through the lens of functionalism, I see the religious pattern of affirming blacks' humanity and advocating a fuller, richer life for African Americans as part of an ongoing existential exercise undertaken by humans in every generation. This task involves asking the perennial questions of meaning and human destiny—quandaries that have preoccupied humans for millennia, perhaps as far back in time as the history of the human species itself. Stephen Mitchell's work on the Gilgamesh myth, one of the oldest surviving narratives available to contemporary humans, comes to mind here. Dating from the early years of the third millennium before the Common Era, this myth centers on the hero's question, "What is my life about?"[27] Ancient Greek tragedians and philosophers were also engaged with such basic questions of existence, asking: "Who do you think you are?" "What do you think should happen?" "Where do you think you come from?" In some traditional African contexts, these questions of identity and personhood have been associated with the ubiquitous concept of *ubuntu*, which has received much attention in the context of post-apartheid South African cultural discourses. As a form of humanism, *ubuntu* connotes for many South African citizens an implied and expected indebtedness of persons to the community that gives them their identities.[28] These cultural examples reveal that the perennial questions of human life, purpose, and meaning, as well as the ongoing task of asking them, have constituted the great myths of philosophy and literature; more importantly, these questions remain the primary focus of most religious traditions. Given its emergence from the historical realities of slavery, black religious expression in the United States brings into relief an important point that white humanists have failed to grasp: black slaves and their descendants have never had the luxury of asking these questions in abstraction. In surviving and making a claim about the value of life, American blacks have lived these questions into the future—both for their contemporaries and for generations to come.

Through the lens of functionalism, there is also the possibility of viewing black religious expression as a specific type of values discourse upheld by individuals and communities in their myriad struggles to humanize their existence. From a naturalistic perspective, all humans are value-laden organisms. As we experience existence, the meaningfulness of that experience is mediated through values discourse. In other words, humans do more than just exist—we actualize ourselves or engage in processes of becoming through subjectivizing the world around us, using the principles, standards, or qualities that inform as well as guide that actualization.[29] Insofar as an evolving black religious tradition has vigilantly affirmed blacks' full humanity amid its emancipatory aims, it has persisted in connecting religiosity with a fundamental propensity toward life. Thus, employing specific images, symbols, and rituals, black religiosity has functioned in the United States to address fundamental issues of life and death for black agents intent on living fully and with dignity. For example, as discussed above, the symbol *God* has often functioned in African American religious culture to affirm the value of black humanity as well as the fact that all humans share in the same ontological reality. Equally important, this concept has been posited as an ultimate value—indeed, an a priori notion—within African American religious thought, symbolizing the means by which particular limitations on human potentiality could be dissolved or at least addressed. What is crucial here is recognizing the creative energies of blacks who rejected the impoverished conceptions of their humanity, which justified slavery, Jim Crow laws, segregation, and other unjust social practices and cultural norms through the last several hundred years.

The preceding examples accentuate the undeniable significance of black religious discourse in promoting processes of transformation. Yet, from my perspective, they also raise an important, more fundamental question for contemporary readers: how should we understand the complex human being who is affirmed in African American liberationist discourse? In my attempt to address this question, I emphasize influential developments in humanistic studies that have shifted attention away from the traditional object of faith (deity) to emphasize human subjectivity. In short, these developments have focused on the human as a proper starting point for understanding religious valuing. These shifts warrant further attention within an African American cultural context, as doing so will help determine the unique placement of the African American religious humanism I advance in this book.

The Rise of Modern Humanism and Some Key Cultural Practices

With a general movement from Immanuel Kant's positioning of morality as the focal point of religion, through Georg W. F. Hegel's speculative idealism, to Friedrich Schleiermacher's elevation of intuition or feeling, during the past several centuries religious thought in the West has placed greater emphasis on human ingenuity, and less on the divine as the transcendent Other. From Cartesianism, through the Enlightenment, to idealism and Romanticism, a shift in imagery arose—attributes traditionally predicated of the divine subject were transferred to the human subject. In other words, as Mark C. Taylor has argued, through a dialectical reversal, the creator God dies and is resurrected as the creative subject.[30] As God created the world through the Logos, so (Western) humanity now creates a world through conscious and unconscious projection. Like the God of classical theology, this sovereign subject relates asymmetrically only to what it constructs and is, therefore, unaffected by anything other than itself. The subject becomes the first principle (formerly identified as God) from which everything arises and to which all must be reduced or returned. Moreover, an undue emphasis on human knowledge eventually leads to a system of thought in which all objects of knowledge exist for the epistemological subject. As Taylor remarks, "If man is defined as subject, everything else turns into object. This includes God, who now becomes merely the highest object of man's knowledge."[31] In areas of knowledge as diverse as science, theology, and early modern philosophy, one locates an essential egoistical faith (albeit directed toward different ends), or an exclusive concern for and interest in humanity. Knowledge in general becomes knowledge for humans, *pro nobis*. While denying God, modern (secular) humanists cling to the autonomous and creative self.

In the late nineteenth and early twentieth centuries, these earlier theoretical developments culminated in (and were best represented by) the Protestant liberal movements derived from the German intellectual tradition. Although too broad and complex to outline here, twentieth-century liberal theology has featured an interesting array of thinkers who have continuously grappled with the role and task of religion in an increasingly complex and troubled world.[32] With the increased attention to epistemological quandaries that modern scientific views have forced on religious thought, many contemporary theologians continued to uncover new foundations on which to establish Christian truths.[33] With one shift focusing on the human subject of faith, modern liberal theology introduced a new problematic within religious scholarship: an attempt to articulate the deep structures of the experiences and consciousness of a self that is said to be representative for all humans. For example, Tillich's existential approach that speaks of human nature in general abstract terms reflects a fundamental flaw in Western reason: its universal and ahistorical tendencies. In a fashion akin to that of modern philosophy, with its obsession with identity and singularity, these types of theological configurations have failed to speak convincingly of the human subject in all its historical complexity. Just as the categories of Western philosophy obliterated differences of gender and race as these shape and structure the experience and subjectivity of the self, a dominant model of modern theological thought posited itself as the discourse of the one self-identical subject, thereby blinding us to (and in fact delegitimizing) the presence of types of otherness and difference that do not fit into its categories. With this insight, one is reminded of the rise of black, feminist, queer, and other liberation theologies or religious critiques in which marginalized histories are taken into account.[34]

The critical trends just mentioned show that influential notions of the human and its spheres of creativity, as represented by this dominant form of modernity, have been ambiguous as well as potentially lethal in their consequences. For example, one dilemma of modernism is that precisely in its creativity and success in enacting its most cherished ideals, Western humanity has brought forth material conditions and an ethos of dominion that threaten its own life as well as that of other sentient beings. Classic Enlightenment ideals such as progress, universalism, and guaranteed freedoms, which were privileged at the end of the eighteenth and throughout the nineteenth century, have also appeared in certain contexts as suspicious ideologies, masking special privileges and selfish materialism. For example, scientific medicine, long viewed as the paradigmatic expression of Enlightenment reason, has been lax regarding matters of general health (and this is further complicated by the race, gender, and class inequalities in health care), as well as burdened by what appears to be an endlessly acquisitive nature. Likewise, technical industrialism, in expanding as the Enlightenment had hoped it would, now poses a threat to myriad natural systems and the depletion of crucial natural resources on which we all depend. Furthermore, the modern era was dominated by a humanistic spirit intent on reducing plurality to oneness and overcoming ambiguity and temporality with certitude and eternal truths. Begun as a revolt against oppressive political and religious structures, enlightened rationality fell short of its emancipatory aims to culminate in reigns of terror, such as the West's colonization and exploitation of various cultures in the Americas, Asia, and Africa and the Nazis' industrialization of murder. Modern technological acquisition, domination, and utilitarianism—now well-established features of modern culture—became the visible marks of a subjectivity possessed by the desire to be in and of itself completely and to control itself completely. With its foundationalism and drive toward epistemology, the modern era produced the idea of the modern human as the secularized god, replacing the classical (male) deity of old—an essentially narcissistic phenomenon.

This modern notion of selfhood contributed to a system of ordering and cultural representation that was entrenched in a certain fear of difference or suspicion of otherness; humanistic knowledge involved identifying and naming oneself by way of differentiating oneself from an-other. In one of its earliest and most recurrent forms, the problem of the other is posed in terms of the relationship between the one and the many, or unity and plurality, which has been the germ of conventional philosophical thinking, resulting in the onto-theological tradition (to use a term aptly coined by Heidegger).[35] In modern humanism, the (normative) self labors to establish its identity, attempting to surmount the threat that the other poses to its autonomy by dissolving alterity and assimilating difference, and perhaps revealing modernity's fear of death.[36] This interplay of identity/difference within the Western social and cultural realms unmasks psychological processes underlying hierarchical and domineering structures of Western thought. The myth of an all-consuming, powerful plenitude actually sustains its privileged position by simultaneously denying (and parasitically sucking the life out of) that to which it is inextricably linked. In keeping with this theme, humanistic atheism became nothing less than the psychology of mastery in which self-assertion functioned to negate material others (those marked by racial, gender, and sexual difference) as well as the divine other.

For our purposes, it is crucial to note that the dominant model of subjectivity arising in modern humanism was a prototypically tyrannical, narcissistic self—replete with gender, racial, and class biases reinforcing problematic differentials—that was strengthened by Enlightenment ideals. As a seductive form of Western cultural hegemony, Enlightenment reasoning collapsed differences of culture, race, and religious orientation into a single, uniform mode of being, valuing, and knowing. As African philosopher Emmanuel Eze has persuasively demonstrated, Enlightenment reasoning provided an ideal intellectual and epistemological basis for establishing and legitimating the hegemony of the West over the other traditions Europeans were beginning to encounter in Asia, Africa, and the Americas.[37] Traditions, values, and folk practices radically different from or not easily compatible with Enlightenment ideals were often viewed suspiciously and assigned lowly positions on the hierarchy of value, beneath the required level of cognition or scientificity.[38]

Ironically enough, liberal humanism, espousing the universal rights of humans—or, as it has most often been posited, the rights of Man—spawned a distinct set of discursive formations and cultural practices that justified unjust capitalist social relations in the West and their extension, via colonialism and imperialism, to other societies. Jean-Paul Sartre depicted the violence of liberal universal discourse when he noted that abstract assumptions of universality have in fact served as a cover for the more down-to-earth practices of slavery, colonialism, racism, barbarity: "Liberty, equality, fraternity, love, honor, patriotism, and what have you. All this did not prevent us from making speeches about dirty niggers, dirty Jews and dirty Arabs."[39] Here Sartre alludes to the development of the Anglo-European construction of whiteness as the normative identity for human subjectivity. This form of racism depended upon a logic of racial difference whereby one group, select Europeans, defined itself as "white" in such a way that it became the standard from which other races or groups were judged, on the basis of the degree to which they were more or less "white." Thus the white liberal subject often identified itself as full, and judged others (those identified as nonwhite) as empty, or existing in a condition of lack. In modernity this condition of lack eventually took on group associations, which often led in anti-black societies to the dichotomy of fullness and hunger taking symbolic form, as lightness and darkness, whiteness and blackness, and—the most complete and extreme form of this racialized binary logic—the construction of the superiority of the white race over the black races. Insights gleaned from recent studies in race theory are important to interject here and are valuable. They show that even though such terms as *blackness* and *whiteness* are constructions that are projected, they take on meanings that apply to certain groups of people in such a way that it becomes difficult to think of those people without certain affectively charged associations. Thus the blackness and whiteness of individuals and groups are regarded by a racist culture, which takes too seriously the associations adhering to these terms, as their essential features—as, in fact, material, biological features of the very being of these individuals and groups.[40]

The Humanistic Mandate and the Reinscription of African American Religiosity

Addressing the adverse effects of this legacy of racialized reason (or reasoned racism) has been one of the hallmarks of African American intellectualism. With varying degrees of conceptual, ethical, and aesthetic astuteness, various thinkers, artists, and leaders have taken up the critical task of stating the truth: African Americans, too, are human. And, as suggested above, the liberationist theme in African American religiosity has been part of the repeated call by black intellectuals, visionaries, and community leaders to conceive of something different. In North America, this theme remains a resilient and necessary act of resistance against the hubris and naivety of Euro-American humanistic thinking—a gesture that seems to have escaped the critical eye of many humanists. I contend that African American religious culture compels us to question the notion of the human that is implicitly affirmed in humanistic reasoning. Thus, at this critical juncture, I see African American religious discourse as both shaped by and yet resisting this influential vein of humanism. With other religious thinkers who have attempted to address the contemporary crisis of meaning ushered in by modern humanistic thought,[41] I also grapple with the value and epistemic clarity of religious thought, once existing conceptions of the world become dubious or lose their plausibility.

In the wake of post-Enlightenment assessments, all attempts to speak of extrahistorical references (often implicit in traditional confessional thought) are thwarted for many of us by the new emphasis on the historical, sociopolitical dimensions of all discourse. Metaphysical speculation is ruled out, as are teleological views of history and universal, abstract notions of human nature. Yet in returning to the theme of liberation in black religious expression, and in affirming its ongoing legacy, I am inspired and rejuvenated by the exciting new intellectual task made possible by these theoretical developments. I contend that if black religiosity has anything important to say about the real, or the sacred, as the hermeneuticists wish to claim, it must address the full complexity of the "human," as at once stubborn materiality and artful textuality. Toward that end, I envision a view of sacred humanity that points to the various endeavors of African Americans to humanize our existence. Here, I am envisioning a neo-Nietzschean move that valorizes the human as a site for understanding religious valuing. With other African American intellectuals and cultural workers, I now ask, in my own idiom: What possible images of *humanness*, perhaps ennobling and dignifying, can we artfully inscript upon the tissues, bones, and liquid of which we are constituted? What does it mean to say that we, too, are human?

Artful Textuality: Reinscripting Black Religiosity

A first critical step toward this task is drawing attention to the processes of meaning, symbolization, and power formation in humanistic discourses.[42] Here, there is a shift in emphasis from an all-knowing, unified, intending subject as the site of production to that of language and its rhetorical effects. As Roland Barthes has suggested, an author is not simply a person but a socially and historically constituted subject existing as a cultural process—what Barthes calls a *scriptor*, and what Foucault will call an *author-function*. The author cannot claim any absolute authority over her text because, in some ways, she did not write it. Any subject who enunciates is a creation of language itself, so that meaning belongs to the play of language and is far beyond individual control. As we acquire language, we enter a flow of meaning with broad cultural implications, so that Foucault can speak, for example, of stepping into the flow of meaning, and Lacan of our entering, through language, into the Law of the Father, the rule of the governing conceptions of our culture. Accordingly, the type of religious discourse that I imagine emerging is one that transforms the current religious scholar into the Barthian scriptor, who is born with the text, at the same time.

This form of textuality also has to do with the fuller conceptions of meaning that accompany a reconceived style of reading, writing, and reflection. One might again recall Barthes' famous assertion: "We know now that a text is not a line of words releasing a single 'theological' meaning (the 'message' of the Author-God) but a multi-dimensional space in which a variety of writings, none of them original, blend and clash."[43] A conception of language as a multivalent system of differentiations and as a depository of cultural meanings and power-inflected gestures resonates well with my own desire to reinscript black religiosity as part of a complex web of cultural meanings, as a texture of them—even as a text. Accordingly, a (religious) text is, to borrow Barth's terms, "a tissue of quotations drawn from the innumerable centres of culture"—a human text that is "written *here* and *now*" rather than after some (theo) author's thought.[44] Hence, I suggest we pay particular attention to the conventions and structures of writing about selfhood and about the human. I also emphasize considering how different models of humanity are conceived and written about, as well as how our humanity is expressed in the process of writing; here, it is also important to take notice of how later texts relate to previous texts, and to consider the ways we speak about various aspects of our human lives and experiences.

The inevitability of each religious scriptor's supplementing—as Derrida might phrase it—already written texts opens possibilities of collective authorship that dismantle the idea of writing that originates from a single, fixed source and results in a single, fixed meaning. Meaning is indefinite and in flux, because signs can only point to other signs. Since we are inside the circle of language, we express its logic, its stereotypes, its rhetorical twists, and its power effects in all we do. Yet while reinventing and participating in distinct forms of disciplinary rhetorical strategies that contribute to the always-ongoing constructions of human knowledge, and while acknowledging the inevitable processes of open-ended textuality, I want to stress a critical point: just as African Americans should not participate in naively essentialist notions of black selfhood, we must be careful not to construct an insufficient subjectivity, in which historical agents are "erased" by linguistic forces over which they can have little or no control. If we do so, we risk losing sight of those aspects of embodied humans that are rooted in intimate and concrete social relations, and of something within and among humans that is not merely an effect of the dominant discourse.

These concerns lead me, as a religious scriptor, to raise a crucial question for contemporary readers and writers of African American religious textuality: What is this "human" that is generally implied or assumed in our cultural observations? I believe that religious discourse involves more than a recognition and description of ordinary human behaviors—it is itself an ongoing, constituted celebration of the conundrums, dreams, and desires of the irreducibly embodied, relational "human." In the next chapter, I address this question as I introduce and establish conceptual grounds for establishing an expanded view of the human within the framework of religious naturalism. In the process of doing so, I reiterate the value and significance of reflecting on Du Bois's prophetic sense of conceiving anew older convictions with new religious ideals. Acknowledging the evolution of African American religiosity and its enduring legacy, I contend, requires us to ask questions about the nature of the human. Furthermore, this quintessential religious query, its import, and perhaps its distinctive role within contemporary American intellectual thought and culture, is a difficult but necessary task.

Sacred Humanity as Stubborn, Irreducible Materiality

The same stream of life that runs through my veins night and day
runs through the world and dances in rhythmic measures. It is
the same life that shoots in joy through the dust of the earth in
numberless blades of grass and breaks into tumultuous waves of
leaves and flowers. It is the same life that is rocked in the ocean-
cradle of birth and of death, in ebb and in flow. I feel my limbs are
made glorious by the touch of this world of life. And my pride is
from the life-throb of ages dancing in my blood this moment.

—RABINDRANATH TAGORE, *Stream of Life*

In unmasking a cultural legacy of problematic racial differentiations, African American and post-Enlightenment cultural critiques vividly remind us that contemporary Westerners are still wrestling with age-old queries regarding our humanity. They also inspire some of us to imagine new possibilities as we engage in current struggles against dehumanizing structures in the United States. The notion of sacred humanity I introduce in this chapter is one of these possibilities. With it, I advance a radical humanism with religious sensibilities that is also supported by scientific ideas and thought. Today, religionists and other humanist scholars are compelled to ascertain new, deeper ways of asking who we humans are, of asking about human purpose and meaning, and of asking about the value of human life—basic questions that are as old as some of our earliest stories, religious sentiments, and philosophies. Not surprisingly, these ancient questions are now part of current rational efforts to understand who we are and our world through scientific means, thereby creating an exciting, critical juncture for humanists. If we overlook the perennial character of such questions, we lose perspective on their importance; yet failing to recognize the contemporary scientific context of these fundamental questions increases the possibility of offering unintelligible or meaningless answers for the lives we actually live today. As Susan Haack has suggested, science represents the "most remarkable amplification and refinement of a [characteristically] human talent, the capacity to inquire."[1]

The capacious notion of sacred humanity I introduce in this chapter is grounded in scientific theories advanced by the tenets of religious naturalism. I envision humanity as a specific life form, or as nature made aware of itself. More specifically, I posit a view of humans as interconnected, social, value-laden organisms in constant search of meaning (cognition), enamored of value (goodness, love, justice), and instilled with a sense of purpose (telos). This naturalistic vision emphasizes deep interconnectedness among humans and our kinship with other sentient life, accentuating humans' propensity toward life. Within the context of African American culture and history, this view of humanity underscores the conceptual richness of the liberationist motif within black religiosity and celebrates its enduring legacy. With the concept of sacred humanity, I thus bring to light newer, deeper understandings of key basic convictions in African American religious expression. Posed rhetorically as questions, these convictions have us asking: What does it means to be human and to affirm the essential value of blacks? How do we continue justifying religiously that indeed all humans share in the same ontological reality? Why do racist conceptions of blacks' inferior humanity still linger, as woefully impoverished and inadequate as they appear in light of current scientific views that show a deep interrelatedness among all biotic life forms? As a means of understanding the religious sentiment of love, how do we continue valuing and celebrating life and the worth of all beings? In asking these questions, I invite all Americans—not just African Americans—to participate in ongoing conversations regarding the quandaries of grasping and sharing certain basic convictions about our common humanity.

In acknowledging a scientific context for articulating specific religious truth claims, I state my preference for naturalistic theories established by religious naturalism over specific trends in cognitive science research (CSR). I am not interested in replicating the reductionist forms of argumentation emerging from such thinkers as Matthew Alper, who considers humans to be religious animals whose brains are hard-wired for "God," even as he asserts that no God exists, and that the "spiritual" is really the "scientific."[2] Among other provocative perspectives is that of Richard Dawkins, who suggests that the predisposition of humans to believe in God is due to the fact that we, like computers, tend to do what we are told. In his discussion of the child brain, for example, Dawkins argues that it has been preprogrammed by natural selection to obey and believe what parents and other adults tell it; for Dawkins, this is generally a favorable thing. He adds, however, that the child brain is also susceptible to infection and mental viruses, especially when it fastens upon the inferior or worthless religious ideas of charismatic preachers and other adults. In other words, for Dawkins, the underside of this phenomenon is that ineffective and deficient ideas (that is, religious ones) can be passed down from one generation to another.[3] Elsewhere, in reference to certain metaphysical religious affirmations, Todd Tremlin contends that supernatural beings are merely mental conceptions that human brains acquire, represent, and transmit as a result of the evolutionary process. As the natural products of human evolutionary psychology, "gods" can be explained scientifically as successful ideas.[4] Further, from an anthropological perspective, Pascal Boyer has argued that recent scientific developments reveal in humanity a central metaphysical urge—an "irredeemable human propensity toward superstition, myth and faith, or a special emotion that only religion provides," which, he believes, stands at the root of all religion.[5]

The key assumptions underlying these forms of CSR often lead to the impoverished conclusion that religious claims are primarily and best understood in psychoanalytical or biological terms, or that religion is ultimately a residual (albeit ineffectual) evolutionary mechanism operating in humanity that *must* be overcome. I am wary of the dogmatic reductionism, ahistoricism, and subtle universalism evident in those who dismiss religion on such terms. In this work, I am not interested in achieving negative determinations about religion that posit in problematic, universal ways its abnormality or irrationality.[6] Moreover, when addressing the symbol *God* in theistic renderings, I have no desire or intent to determine conclusively whether or not an objective, real being actually corresponds to humans' construction of it; I believe our intellectual energies are much better served in shifting attention away from the endless intellectual posturing involved in asking whether or not a transcendental subject exists, or even whether one can establish an empirical basis for deciding whether it exists. Rather, I prefer to focus on explorations of the human, or on that which I perceive as much more demonstrably knowable—or, at least, as an object of study that is easier to speculate or theorize about than particular conceptions of transcendental ideals—with the aid of current forms of knowledge. In so doing, I align myself with other naturalists who see the religious potential in our scientific understandings of nature, including scientific views of the human organism.

Religious Naturalism: Reinscripting the Human as Stubborn Materiality

Scholars often trace the historical roots of religious naturalism back to Spinoza (1632–1677) and identify its corpus with a wide range of thinkers. These include naturalist philosopher George Santayana; Mordecai Kaplan, founder of Reconstructionist Judaism in the 1930s; Henry Nelson Wieman and Bernard Meland, proponents of the mid-twentieth-century Chicago school of empirical process theology; and contemporary cell biologist Ursula Goodenough.[7] At the heart of religious naturalism in all of its variants is a basic conviction: any truths we are ever going to discover, and any meaning in life we should uncover, are revealed to us through the natural order. In this study, I embrace a contemporary strain of religious naturalism within the science and religion paradigm that is best associated with the works of Goodenough, Donald Crosby, and Loyal Rue, all of whom have been influential in my development as a religious naturalist.[8] This vein of religious naturalism is appealing to me because in focusing on the materiality of existence, it has also included human nature and human culture in its grasp of naturalism; in doing so, it is challenging some widely held paradigms about the nature of "nature." Another attractive feature of this strain of religious naturalism is its emphasis on emergence as an important new concept for thinking about biological and cosmic evolution. Consider, for example, that emergent properties arise as a consequence of relationships—for instance, the relationships between water molecules that generate a snowflake, or the relationships between neurons that generate a memory. Emergent properties also give rise to yet more emergent properties, generating the vast complexity of our present-day cosmic, biological, ecological, and cultural contexts.[9] These insights compel us to reflect meaningfully on the emergence of matter (and especially life) from the Big Bang forward, promoting an understanding of myriad nature as complex processes of becoming. The general view of humanity I hold, on which I build my concept of sacred humanity, arises from this context. With other religious naturalists, I believe that understanding the deep history of the cosmos is profoundly important for any basic understanding of the materiality of being human, being alive in the manner we currently find ourselves. Humans are highly complex organisms, owing the lives we have to the emergence of hierarchies of natural systems. Expressed succinctly by Rue, humans are "ultimately the manifestations of many interlocking systems—atomic, molecular, biochemical, anatomical, ecological—apart from which human existence is incomprehensible."[10]

Human life is also part of an evolutionary history showing directionality, or a trend toward greater complexity and consciousness. As Stephen J. Gould and other scientists have noted, there has been an increase in the genetic information in DNA, and a steady advance in the ability of organisms to both gather and process information about the environment and respond to it.[11] Goodenough has provided a persuasive view of evolutionary theory that celebrates such directionality, and her descriptive account of how life works in terms of biophysics and biochemistry is useful here: "life, we can now say, is getting something to happen against the odds and remembering how to do it. That something that happens is biochemistry and biophysics, the odds are beat by intricate concatenations of shape fits and shape changes, and the memory is encoded in genes and their promoters."[12] Biophysics is concerned with "electrochemical gradients" and the physics through which "channels and pumps" work to "span the cell membrane" and thus allow the chemical processes of the cell to work.[13] Basic biochemistry has to do with the shapes of proteins, particularly enzymes, and the sequences of shape changes or cascades, that is, those processes through which a cell perceives or interacts with that which is external to it. Accordingly, as Goodenough affirms, the "cell is set up to optimize the flowing of cascades": that is, proteins that will interact with one another have "domains, called addresses, that target the proteins to the same cellular location" and each "destination proves optimal for particular biochemical reactions."[14] This means that a cell is like a community: its inner workings are segregated into interacting compartments, whereas its outer membrane defines its interactions with the rest of the world.

Biochemistry and biophysics generate the patterns that constitute pulsating organisms, including the development of multicellular organisms such as humans. To understand this idea fully, it is important to grasp the concept of natural selection and its role in our evolutionary heritage as human animals. As Goodenough points out, minimally, evolution can be viewed as changes in the frequencies of different sets of instructions for making organisms. To understand evolution, then, one must grasp how the instructions become different (mutation), and then how the frequencies of occurrence of particular instructions are changed (natural selection). Within the context of describing mutation as simply a change in the sequence of nucleotides in a genome, the concept of natural selection raises two important questions: Does the new protein or promoter work better, worse, or the same as the old one? How important is this difference to the organism?[15] The dynamic processes of evolution occur through chains of modification—a protein is slightly modified by a mutation; this modification gets further modified or added to, and eventually, over time, complex new systems emerge. For example, bacteria flagella started out with a protein to improve acid transport that happened to also rotate; even though the rotation was originally an irrelevant consequence, this feature was eventually built onto as other proteins attached to it, and so on. In this context, the term *bricolage* (the construction of things using what is at hand, similar to how one makes a patchwork quilt) is a colorful and helpful metaphor to help us grasp the complex process.[16] Following Goodenough's lead, I also offer the metaphor of music as a useful bridge for understanding the complexities of evolution. Consider, for example, how a good musicologist can often detect older forms or variations (a fugal texture, a specific cadence, or even a melodic strain) in new compositions. This music analogy helps describe the complexity of evolutionary life, too, as a fascinating organic composition of intricate movements in which the old is woven with the new to generate something more. Goodenough observes:

> A good biochemical idea—a protein domain that binds well to a promoter, a channel that's just the right size for a calcium ion—gets carried along through time, tweaked and modulated to best serve the needs of the current composition/organism but recognizable through evolutionary history. These conserved ideas combine with novelty to generate new direction, new ways of negotiating new environmental circumstances.[17]

This technical scientific discussion inspires a rich, even poetic, rendering of human life as one distinct biotic form emerging from, and participating in, a series of evolutionary processes that constitute the diversity of life. Additionally, and significantly, in this study the scientific epic becomes the starting point for positing an African American religious humanism constituted by a central tenet: humans are relational processes of nature; in short, as stated above, we are nature made aware of itself. In declaring such, I contend that our *humanity* is not a given, but rather an achievement. Consider that from a strictly biological perspective, humans are organisms that have slowly evolved from earlier primates by a process of natural selection. From one generation to another, the species that is alive now has gradually adapted to changing environments so that it could continue to survive. Our animality, from this perspective, is living under the influence of genes, instincts, and emotions, with the prime directive to survive and procreate. Yet this minimalist approach fails to consider what a few cognitive scientists and most philosophers, humanists, and religionists tend to accentuate: our own personal experience of what it is like to be an experiencing human being. Becoming human, or actualizing ourselves as human beings, in this sense, emerges out of an awareness and desire to be more than a conglomeration of pulsating cells. It is suggesting that our humanity is not reducible to organizational patterns or processes dominated by brain structures; nor do DNA, diet, behavior, and the environment solely structure it. Human animals become human destinies when we posit fundamental questions of value, meaning, and purpose to our existence. Our coming to be human destinies is structured by a crucial question: How do we come to terms with life?

With other religious naturalists, I share the sentiment that reveling in a sense of our connectedness with other living beings can only be described as sacred. On the molecular level, there is evidence to support the loftier (or religious) idea that in the very nature of life itself there is some essential joining force. This orientation toward joining with others in establishing our common humanity is what I imagine when using the phrase *sacred humanity*. Humans are, by our very constitution, relational, and our wholeness occurs within a matrix of complex interconnectedness; in this context, our sacrality has fundamentally to do with ways of conjoining with others that transform us. Granted, this is not your typical approach to the *sacred*, which admittedly is a complex word that has been used for a wide range of phenomena: places, time, persons, events, and deities. Traditionally, when people designate something as sacred, they view the thing in question as "other than ordinary." Thus, in the broadest sense of the term, the sacred has been used by scholars, especially those sympathetic to the work of Mircea Eliade, to convey the extraordinary.[18] While I share Eliade's sense that the term *sacred* is not tradition-specific, I reject his sense that the sacred is necessarily grounded in a supernatural reality or a transcendent order. As a naturalist, I am perplexed by a view of the sacred as the manifestation of a wholly different, transcendent order, or as a reality that neither belongs to nor fundamentally inheres within all that is part of our natural, "profane" world. Rather, my usage of the term *sacred* is imbued with the quality of ultimacy within the confines of what religious naturalism affirms: nature as the realm in which we move, live, and have our being.

According to my view, sacrality is a specific affirmation and appreciation of that which is fundamentally important in life, or that which is ultimately valued: relational nature. Humans are interconnected parts and processes of nature, and our sacrality is a given part of nature's richness, spectacular complexity, and beauty. Notwithstanding the diverse cultural and individual approaches to articulating this truth, there is for me, quite simply, an awe-filled affirmation of deep human interconnectedness and complex entangledness with all that is. Finding meaning and value in our lives within the natural order presupposes this fundamental interconnect-edness. Moreover, we can claim and become our humanity in seeking and finding community with others—and with otherness. This is a simple value that religious discourse has advanced and reiterated again and again. Goodenough writes:

> We have throughout the ages sought connection with higher powers
> in the sky or beneath the earth, or with ancestors in some other realm.
> We have also sought, and found, religious fellowship with one another.
> And now we realize that we are connected to all creatures. Not just
> in food chains or ecological equilibria. We share a common ancestor.
> We share genes for receptors and cell cycles and signal-transduction
> cascades. We share evolutionary constraints and possibilities. We are
> connected all the way down.[19]

The basic conception of the human as an emergent, interconnected life-form amid spectacular biotic diversity has far-reaching implications within the context of African American culture. As stated earlier, African American religiosity helped establish an intellectual legacy that has attempted to overcome the deficient conceptions of our humanity couched in prob-lematic racial constructions. Furthermore, this lineage of African American religious thought has aided other discourses in unmasking the self-congratulatory proclamations of the West's post-Enlightenment ideals (or modern humanism) as fraudulent claims that can lead to acts of genocide. This body of thought provides the impetus and vision for my formula-tion of sacred humanity in the twenty-first century. Minimally, and at face value, *sacred humanity* is an apt descriptor of African Americans intent on humanizing their existence in the face of dehumanizing gestures and tac-tics by dominant white culture. Its wider applicability is evident on another level. The term conceptually presupposes all human beings as biotic forms emerging from evolutionary processes sharing a deep homology with other sentient beings and also valuing such connection. As such, it can be used to challenge the most viral constructions of "isms" rooted in problematic and alienating self/other differentiations, especially the racially constructed ones that the enduring legacy of African American religiosity has targeted. Any inkling of white supremacy, or sense of cultural superiority of any ilk, is antithetical to this natural view; these skewed cultural constructions are forced impositions on the wholeness of natural interrelatedness and the deep genetic homology that evolution has wrought.

Within the context of American racial discourse that has persistently placed blacks outside of the circle of humanity, the notion of sacred humanity symbolizes the rejection of seeing our humanity solely as an individualistic phenomenon; some type of communal ontology is implied. A crucial lesson here is that notwithstanding the cultural and national differences and specificities we construct, humans are all genetically connected and part of a greater whole; any harm done to another human is essentially harm done to ourselves. No less important is appreciating how the concept of sacred humanity operates within religious naturalism to emphasize myriad layers of entanglement and essential connectivity—with oneself, one's family, the larger human community, myriad local and global ecosystems, and, yes, the universe. Religiously, this implies love, and love implies concern for the well-being of the beloved. The concept of sacred humanity thus reinforces perennial, expansive perspectives from the wisdom traditions that adamantly promote kindness, empathy, and compassion for all natural processes, including human ones. With the capacity to influence one another and other natural processes, humans have a responsibility to act in ways that promote the flourishing of all life, and to urge other humans who may be less inclined toward our interconnectedness to do the same.

As the liberationist theme in African American religiosity has attempted to articulate in more traditional terms, this sense of our embeddedness within matrixes of complex relationality challenges the denigrative self/ other distinction operative in cultural forms of violence perpetuated by separatist ideologies. It alerts us to the fact us that our mutual relationality has been overshadowed by a dominant view of the self (or being) as separate from that which it perceives as the other (or nonbeing). As noted earlier, this view of the human self has successfully undergirded a legacy of dualism emanating from the Cartesian-inspired worldview that has helped to justify hierarchical and asymmetrical relationships found within our prevailing cultural practices. In historical, social, and philosophic terms, this influential, logical structure of dualism has been characterized by the denial of interdependency, and by alienated forms of differentiation and representations of otherness—all of them conceptual entrapments that varied feminists, ecologists, and postcolonial thinkers have resisted. Unfortunately, the effects of this dualistic worldview linger in those who still view reality in terms of a whole chain of dualistic relations—soul/body, spirit/matter, culture/nature, male/female, human/animal, white/black, rich/poor, straight/gay—in which the second half of each pair is seen as alien and subject to the first.

Sacred Humanity and Meaningful Existence

I am aware that any attempt to derive an African American religiosity based on an understanding of humans as natural processes may seem troublesome to some. One may recall, for example, that nineteenth-century scientific perspectives on natural processes within later evolutionary thought (the new "science of man") promoted Enlightenment racism, in which notions of racial differences often led a perception of the social inequalities between various cultural groups as reflecting the prescripts of nature.[20] However, these ideological extensions are part of a discourse on nature that some contemporary feminists, religious scholars, and postcolonial critics are currently addressing. In resisting these problematic tendencies, my notion of sacred humanity within the framework of religious naturalism also leads us to other possibilities, visions, and assumptions as we continue questioning the idea of Enlightenment progress as well as the ethics of unrestrained development as a means of dominating nature in all its forms.

Religious naturalism offers distinct approaches to the concept of nature that proclaim (in a host of ways) our subjectivities as value-laden nature. It shows that the evolutionary narrative has also propelled humans' efforts to create meaning and purpose in the here and now. This is another crucial aspect of the sacred humanity concept I develop here, one that converges with Rue's descriptive account of human beings as star-born, earth-formed creatures endowed by evolutionary processes to seek reproductive fitness under the guidance of biological, psychological, and cultural systems that have been selected for their utility in mediating adaptive behaviors. Humans maximize their chances for reproductive fitness by managing the complexity of these systems in ways that are conducive to the simultaneous achievement of personal wholeness and social coherence. As Rue states:

> The meaning of human life should be expressed in terms of how our particular species pursues the ultimate telos of reproductive fitness. Like every other species, we seek the ultimate biological goal according to our peculiar nature. That is, by pursuing the many teloi that are internal to our behavior mediation systems, whether these teloi are built into the system by genetic means or incorporated into them by symbolic means. For humans there are many immediate teloi, including the biological goals inherent in drive systems, the psychological goals implicit in our emotional and cognitive system, and the social goals we imbibe through our symbolic systems. Human life is about whatever these goals are about.[21]

My notion of sacred humanity offers a capacious view of our human-ity. Grounded in scientific studies, it emphasizes the social character of cognition in animals and humans, providing various types of evidence for understanding human beings as symbol makers, as creators of a world im-bued with value, and as social organisms. In *The Humanizing Brain*, for example, Carol Albright and James Ashbrooke use Paul MacLeane's no-tion of the tripartite brain to argue that the limbic system, which we share with all other mammals, is the center of emotions that mobilize action and makes possible rich forms of relationship that involve empathy and caring for the young.[22] These factors, in turn, lead us to recognize emotion, social relationships, and values often associated with traditional religious sym-bols as part of human reality. Albright and Ashbrooke go on to theorize about the role of the neocortex, as it is developed in primates and humans, as the center of interpretation, organization, symbolic representation, and rationality. While some critics of MacLeane have argued that the relation-ships between the three regions of the brain are more complex than he has recognized, they acknowledge that a distinction of three functions of the brain might still lead to some of the assumptions outlined by Ashbrooke and Albright.

According to Terrence Deacon, what is particularly interesting about the course of human evolution is that it has entailed the co-evolution of three emergent modalities—brain, symbolic language, and culture—with each feeding into and responding to the other two and generating particularly complex patterns and outcomes. In *The Symbolic Species*, he explores the in-tricate connection between the evolution of human language and our brains, or what he calls their co-evolution.[23] The basic gist of Deacon's study is that language itself was part of the process that was responsible for the evolu-tion of the brain. Language has changed the environments in which brains have evolved. We are a species that has been shaped in part by symbols, in part by what we do. According to Deacon, ritual and mythology—simply ways of doing things that are organized conventionally, symbolically—are hallmarks of our species. Humans have reinterpreted and even trans-formed much of our biology through this symbolic system. So much of what we do—marriage, for example, and the expression of conflict through warfare—has been transformed by language that this linguistic tool has, in a sense, taken over and biased all of our interactions with the world. Expressed succinctly, our brain has evolved very differently in some regards from the brains of other species, in ways that are uniquely human.[24]

Based on these insights from Deacon and other scientists, we can af-firm that humans seek meaning by viewing their lives within a cosmic and religious framework that is itself a human symbolic construct—the brain is part of the cosmos and a product of the cosmos. Its structures reflect the nature of the cosmos and whatever ordering and meaning-giving forces are expressed in its history.[25] Another way of stating this is to emphasize that processes of religious valuing within humans are inextricably connected to the fact that we are organisms with built-in values. Evolutionary biologists, sociobiologists, evolutionary psychologists, and philosophers are currently debating the extent to which one can argue that humans are value-driven decision systems with primary values built in. A consistent scientific view is that a successful life outcome consists of promoting the transmission of information conducive to maintaining the emergent dynamic logic that gives life its meaning—that is, promoting the production of emergent outcomes (called traits in biology) that collectively make their own continuation more likely. As Goodenough and Deacon assert:

> Traits common to all organisms include such non-depressing and religiously fertile capacities as end-directedness and identity maintenance; traits common to all animals include awareness and the capacity for pleasure and suffering; traits common to social beings include cooperation and meaning making; traits common to birds and mammals include bonding and nurturance; traits common to humans include language and its capacity to share subjective experiences, and thus to know love. Transmission of genomes is the steady background drumbeat; emergence is the music.[26]

The human self emerges as a biological process that is affected by genes but also by many other factors at higher levels. In human development, as in evolutionary history, selfhood is always social, a product of language, culture, and interpersonal interaction as well as genetic expression. In the gene-culture co-evolution theory (also called dual inheritance theory, or DIT), human behavior is viewed as a product of the interaction of two evolutionary processes, biology and culture. Herbert Gintis, a proponent of this theory, holds that genetic and cultural evolution interacted in the evolution of *Homo sapiens*. DIT recognizes that the natural selection of genotypes is an important component of the evolution of human behavior and that cultural traits can be constrained by genetic imperatives. However, the theory also recognizes that genetic evolution has endowed the human species with a parallel evolutionary process of cultural evolution.[27] DIT has led some religious naturalists to suggest that the genes and cultural memes that constitute the human self interact very much like a violin and a violin composition. You cannot have music without both elements coming together into a seamless whole. In the same way, humans are a seamless whole of genes and culture—their "music."[28]

The point of introducing these various scientific explanations is clear: naturalistic views of the human indicate a complex social organism that can love, connect deeply with others, and symbolize its environment (or engage in world formation) through values and language. Not only that, these explanations lend support to my view of human individuals as multilevel psychosomatic unities—both biological organisms and responsible selves. Another crucial component of being human is the heightened awareness of our ability to make decisions self-consciously, to act on those decisions, and to take responsibility for them.[29] Within the context of blacks' lived experiences in the United States, these insights point to the significance of the liberationist theme in black religiosity: African Americans' tenacious refusal to reduce various actions to mere brute existence (or, rather, to determinist forces and mechanistic explanations of cause and effect). I also associate this impulse with blacks' ability to reflect upon the past, to assess the present, and, inevitably, to consider the future. In the next section, I explore this idea further through the notion of religious valuing.

Sacred Humanity and Religious Valuing

The concept of sacred humanity is a particular configuration of our humanity that celebrates it as a finite organism; as such, it inevitably raises important issues concerning how humans come to terms with the facticity of nonexistence, or, more popularly expressed, with the inevitability of death. It is this angle, I believe, that generates the fullest philosophic and religious connotations of sacred humanity. It is also what distinguishes my model of religious naturalism from strict reductionist forms of naturalism. Religious naturalism posits a view of the human organism as a valuing entity; in this context, I suggest that affirming death also becomes the proper point of departure for appreciating the value and meaningfulness of human life. In advancing this perspective, I follow the general ideas of Konstantin Kolenda in his largely overlooked text, *Religion without God*.[30] In this work, Kolenda transforms the life-death dialectic within the framework of recognizing death as a necessary condition of humans having a destiny. For example, rather than posit a life-death contrast, one may think of these two contrasting terms as necessary conditions for the emergence and development of individual destinies.[31] Hence, for Kolenda, the idea of destiny carries with it the notion of wholeness. And, rather than assume, as many still do, that the ultimate destiny of every human is to die, Kolenda refocuses attention on the fact that the destiny of a human also includes all that he or she has experienced and will experience in life.[32] This insight encourages humans to immerse ourselves in our finite naturalness, and to see that death is not an experience or phenomenon of oppositional otherness.

Human life as a totality is captured more correctly when one understands death as a necessary condition of having a destiny. Another aspect of this theory is that the universe acquires distinct meaning through human destinies. There is a sense of the universe coming to be in a different way with the entrance of human destinies, for "every upsurge of consciousness through the birth of a person" is a triumph (for the universe) and a privilege (for the emerging individual).[33] Following Kolenda's lead, I affirm each human birth as a glorious event, and the starting point of yet another spectacular phenomenon that helps transform the enigmatic cosmos into an even more vital, dramatic world for sentient beings. Consequently, when we value human life and find it interesting or even precious, we are aware of the myriad possibilities and opportunities to light up the cosmos with the varied and seemingly inexhaustible projects of human individuals and cultures.[34] I am not suggesting that the knowable universe is enlivened only through human activity, as that idea retains too much of the hubris of traditional humanism, devaluing the emergence of other forms of animal and plant life, as well as their concomitant levels of sentience, conscious awareness, and valuing. Rather, I am much more compelled by the subtler notion that humans are individual and collective destinies engaging an appreciable world. These ideas help us to view humans as natural organisms that add a particular dimension of value to an already vital, expansive universe.

Speaking of the human experiencer having an experience, or what has been identified as the subjective dimension of experience, implies a theory of consciousness.[35] In the contemporary era, theorists in the science of mind have debated whether or not consciousness can be fully explained. While some have argued that the problem is irresolvable and no good explanation can be given, others state that consciousness is an ambiguous term, referring to many different phenomena, each of which needs to be explained. For example, David Chalmers has classified the associated problems of consciousness as "hard" ones and "easy" ones, describing the latter as responsive to the standard methods of cognitive science and the former as resistant to them.[36] Mental phenomena associated with the hard problems are not easily explained in terms of computational or neural mechanisms, as are those processes related to our ability to discriminate, integrate information, report mental states, focus attention, and so forth. While acknowledging that a whirl of information processing is taking place when we think and perceive, Chalmers notes that there is also a subjective aspect to thinking and perceiving, which he identifies as the *qualia* of experience. As he puts it:

> This subjective aspect is experience. When we see, for example, we *experience* visual sensations: the felt quality of redness, the experience of dark and light, the quality of depth in a visual field. Other experiences go along with perception in different modalities: the sound of a clarinet, the smell of mothballs. Then there are bodily sensations, from pains to orgasms; mental images that are conjured up internally; the felt quality of emotion, and the experience of a stream of conscious thought. What unites all of these states is that there is something it is like to be in them. All of them are states of experience.[37]

With the contention that consciousness cannot be explained exclusively by physical events in the brain, Chalmers and others explicitly reject the reductionism endemic to modern materialistic conceptions of natural phenomena. John R. Searle has described the effects of this legacy of materialistic thinking on the part of the scientific and philosophical communities:

> It would be difficult to exaggerate the disastrous effects that the failure to come to terms with the subjectivity of consciousness has had on the philosophical and psychological work of the past half century. In ways that are not at all obvious on the surface, much of the bankruptcy of most work in the philosophy of mind and a great deal of the sterility of academic psychology over the past fifty years . . . . have come from a persistent failure to recognize and come to terms with the fact that the ontology of the mental is an irreducibly first-person ontology.[38]

Here, it is helpful to consider a view of human destiny in light of Chalmer's description of this ontology of subjective experience. Human lives take on special meanings through our experiences. Even more so, our lives take on meaning and value as they are being filled out, or as we experience ourselves experiencing each moment of existence. The concept of destiny operates here as a wonderful reminder that sole emphasis on the processes associated with the easy problems of consciousness may be a distortion of the stream of life that constitutes our fuller experience as conscious beings. Granted, fragmentation is inevitable because consciousness involves focusing on defining, identifying, and even selecting an item out from its surrounding context. Yet there is a limitation to understanding ourselves as valuers of life when we merely concentrate on isolated moments, or that of an "I" observing an "it." The result, Kolenda notes, is "a staccato effect, a series of static forms or snapshots that do not connect into a flowing, continuous whole."[39] Here, Kolenda's view of the essential three-dimensionality of time comes to mind, as it reminds us that consciousness not only breaks up but also connects its objects. Following his lead, I view human consciousness, minimally, as a constant shuttling to and fro between aspects of lived experience, creating a connectedness of various strands and components of awareness. The value and meaning of an experience arises out of its connection to the past and future; yet only by holding all three aspects together and seeing their interconnections can we fully appreciate what is going on in and around us. When an individual allows the concept of destiny to occupy the center of her self-consciousness, she is in a position to recognize that there is more to her life than the tendency of thought to break up experience into isolated fragments. This amounts to a sense or felt quality within human life that speaks to our experience as valuers. In short, the notion of life as destiny suggests that we recognize the unique value that comes from apprehending the qualitative dimensions of experience.

The relationship between the universe and humans has significance here, as well, because one may plausibly postulate that the universe has value only for valuers. From the perspective of asking whether anything is good or meaningful, one is assuming that such a value judgment cannot be made without a reference to a consciousness making such a judgment. As a center of consciousness, each individual human destiny arises out of the midst of the world and is supported by its structure and history; therefore, it necessarily adds another dimension of value to the cosmos. For religious naturalists like myself, there is no need for a god-figure to help humans make sense of our relationship to the universe. Each human destiny as a distinct valuing process is individually unique and unrepeatable, and, in this sense, each human life is a statement, or a declaration of what the universe can become, as the valuational verdict is different in each case. The crux of the matter is recognizing that so long as an individual's life is ongoing, a final verdict on the meaningfulness of that individual's life cannot be delivered; a coherent statement cannot be made so long as we are living out of a particular center of consciousness. Thus finitude is a logical requirement for meaning, and ultimate meaning is forever in suspense, uncompleted, and incapable of being completed. This is one reason why every human being can regard his or her personal identity as a unique and irreplaceable contribution to myriad cosmic meanings.[40]

Finally, with each human being viewed as a unique destiny, I impress on myself the notion that when I meet a person, I am encountering another center of value. Moreover, assuming that the values realized in human lives are the highest values we know of, then even seeing a stranger on the street puts me face to face with a manifestation of myriad cosmic meanings—both potential and actual. Personal interaction with another becomes an intersection of worlds, as well as our participation in the drama of life in its evolving transformation and expansion. Each human destiny is a recipient of modes of acting, speaking, and thinking that reach deep into the past; here, one may become aware of concrete links with other members of the human race who have prepared the emergence of our destinies by living out theirs. Seen from this perspective, my individual experience is a continuation, a development of a larger emergent project of life itself, and I can view myself as its partial actualization. More eloquently, you and I are important aspects of the evolving, unfolding stream of life.

Sacred Humanity, Human Destinies, and African American Religiosity

This theory of human destinies lends itself to a deepening understanding of religiosity grounded in an appreciable view of our basic human nature. Accordingly, as human destinies, we seek compensation, rounding out the actual with the ideal, according to our talents, insights, and abilities. As I interpret these ideas within the context of African American religious life, I consider such awareness and desire as instances of existential courage. This experience of black religiosity (both individually and culturally) is inextricably connected to how African Americans *become* our humanity—how we literally become human from the perspective of a dominant culture that has denied us that right. Both within the specifics of African American historical and cultural realities, and on a more general level, the sacred humanity I have described in this chapter is that of embodied, value-laden social organisms in constant search of meaning, enamored of value, and instilled with a sense of purpose.

The liberationist theme in African American religiosity is the uncontestable recognition of our longing to take our highest ideals or values seriously: the irrefutable, essential value and beauty of our humanity. The very presence of this desire in African American culture attests to an awareness or sense of distance between what we are and what white supremacy suggests we are, or between the world as it is and as it could be. In short, African Americans have been compelled to seek realms of possibility. This ongoing task—of necessarily positing and celebrating African Americans as humans, and as having the right to become our humanity—has been one way, among many, for African American visionaries to contest impoverished models of black animality conceived by cultural spin doctors mesmerized by distorted racial constructs.

Both within and beyond the specifics of black culture, part of this task of all human organisms becoming our humanity involves the recognition that participation in human affairs helps to transform isolated individual destinies—we become enriched by diverse allegiances, identifications, and loyalties. A major value of this model of African American religious humanism is that it emphasizes humans as relational natural organisms—we are part of the evolving universe, and those values that we confer upon events are more or less the universe appreciating dimensions of itself. This process is not merely narcissistic introspection, isolating any one of us from the contexts in which we live our destinies. Granted, all action, all reality, is for the concrete, material individual: I, right now, where I am. But the process is akin to discovering worlds of possibility beyond the sterile fear of nonexistence, beyond enforced solitariness founded on illusions of separateness and universal abstractions.

In *Enfleshing Freedom: Body, Race, and Being*, M. Shawn Copeland suggests that being human is neither hypothetical nor abstract. Rather, while advancing a theological anthropology based on critical analysis of the body—physical and social, enfleshed, historical, and concrete—and in particular the bodies of black women, Copeland points to an expanded view of selfhood that is concrete, visceral, and embodied in everyday experience and relationships—all determinants of who we are.[41] Ascertaining this fuller sense of humanity evokes the speech of Miranda in *The Tempest* envisioning an enchanted new world of possibility:

O wonder! How many goodly creatures are there here!

How beauteous mankind is! O brave new world! That has such people in it![42]

In light of the emerging theory I advance here, we might now say, "Oh what wondrous worlds that honor such entangled creatureliness—our becoming humans!"

As I mentioned earlier, human life as a totality is captured more correctly when one understands death as a necessary condition for having a destiny, or for being a whole. Thus, our sacrality is inextricably tied to our sense of finitude, which is only possible and truthful when we rest confidently in our natural, material bodies. The holiness of life is recognizing that each moment of existence is an opportunity to honor our finite, stubborn materiality, or our deep homology within a complex network of processes that are part of our becoming human destinies.

In the next chapter, I further explore and trace intimations of this religious ideal within the context of African American intellectual thought. More specifically, I identify key aspects of the sacred humanity concept within select writings of three iconic figures, Anna Julia Cooper, James Baldwin, and W. E. B. Du Bois, whose collective insights date from the late nineteenth century to the middle of the twentieth century. Although none of these writers espouses the full theoretical framework of religious naturalism that I do, I explore how their writings foreshadow key elements of my concept of sacred humanity. In 1892, for example, Anna Julia Cooper's collection of feminist essays and speeches, *A Voice from the South*, challenged the different ways African Americans were systematically dehumanized and denaturalized as the other—categorized below the normative European model of humanity. Cooper assessed the failings of a purportedly enlightened nation that had lost its soul, pointing to its limitations when tested within the crucible of race relations. Cooper rejected the narrow focus of this atomistic outlook and envisioned an ideal American culture, one that inspired and enabled each person to attain fullness of being and to flourish as part of the whole. Her humanistic discourse was grounded in a communal ontology that led her to astutely and wittingly remind her contemporaries of a crucial point: "the philosophic mind sees that its own 'rights' are the rights of humanity."[43] In the same era, Du Bois's conceptualization of life behind the veil of race and the resulting "double-consciousness—a sense of always looking at one's self through the eyes of others" fueled his aspirations for African Americans to look anew at themselves and to reinvent themselves.[44] A few decades later, during a critical period of the civil rights era, James Baldwin also emphatically rejected the distortions of modern humanistic discourse, replacing it with a fuller, more capacious model of humanity. In his essays and works of nonfiction, Baldwin described the sheer ontological weightiness of having to reinvent (or to justify) one's humanity over and over again, in every generation.[45] As is the case with Cooper and Du Bois, Baldwin's published work and activism show the tenacity of African Americans' intellectual and creative engagement with an age-old task: knowing and claiming one's humanity.

Each of these thinkers confronted the persuasive cultural force of a dualistically based worldview and pointed to its far-reaching effects, including the dominant, impoverished view of black bodies as the immoral, devalued other. Taken together, their brave efforts show that when black-ness has been defined narrowly or negatively marked as different, the more capacious vision I elaborate, our sacred humanity, becomes marred and distorted. Their ideas promoted the humanity of African Americans at historical junctures when it was questioned and denied. But their varied emancipatory impulses directed toward forms of racial and social justice are not merely sociocultural expressions. When read from the conceptual framework I have just outlined, their ideas can also be viewed as creative articulations of religiousness that are commensurate with the processual forms of life I identify with the concept of sacred humanity. Interpreting their ideas and works from such a perspective—humans constructing and embracing our humanity—demonstrates the emergence of the African American religious naturalism I explore in this work.

CHAPTER 3

Anna Julia Cooper: Relational Humanity and the Interplay of One and All

A *People* is but the attempt of many
To rise to the completer life of one.

The common *Problem*, yours, mine, every one's
Is—not to fancy what were fair in life
Provided it could be,—but, finding first
What may be, then find how to make it fair
Up to our means; a very different thing!

—ROBERT BROWNING, *Luria*, and "Bishop Blougram's Apology," quoted by Anna Julia Cooper in *A Voice from the South* (Cooper's emphases)

A major feature of the sacred humanity concept I introduced in the last chapter is how inextricably entangled our human lives are as we strive to actualize ourselves as processes of nature. Equally important, this religious notion establishes human beings as sacred centers of value and distinct movements of nature itself in which deep relationality and interconnectedness become key metaphors for understanding what constitutes our processes of becoming human. In this chapter, I explore aspects of these salient features in the writings of Anna Julia Cooper, a former slave and an educator, whose personal experiences in North America inflected her wide range of scholarly interests and activism. Within the last decade, Cooper's life as an educational reformer, feminist theorist, and intellectual has attracted much scholarly interest, including new assessments of her dissertation on the international power struggles over race, her innovative education reforms, and her early model of intersectional feminist discourse.[1] I specifically focus on the collection of Cooper's essays and speeches published as *A Voice from the South* (1892), in which she envisions the ideal of an American culture that would inspire and enable each person to attain fullness of being and to flourish as a part of the whole. Although the volume does not represent a systematic philosophic endeavor, a close reading of select essays reveals Cooper using richly textured ideas, organic imagery, and other rhetorical tropes to outline a dynamic, processual view of American life as a relational whole in which the destinies of "one and all" are inextricably bound together. Cooper develops this theme of a relational whole to challenge racism, sexism, and other discriminatory practices in America, advising the nation that its success depends on how well all its parts can flourish and pursue happiness or self-fulfillment. Furthermore, in conceiving the nation as a relational whole, Cooper explores similarities existing among and between different genders, cultures, races, and emancipatory efforts in nineteenth-century America that were often overlooked by others. It was precisely the intersection of Cooper's social status, historic position, and intellectual interests that resulted in such activism.

Cooper's use of naturalistic images and rhetorical tropes shows the capacious nature of her intellectual vision. After providing a brief introduction to her unique feminist voice in the nineteenth century, I examine Cooper's view of America as a relational whole in which one and all are tied together, emphasizing her use of evolutionary, dynamic imagery befitting natural processes to portray national transformation and promise. Notable here are Cooper's compelling ethical mandates to the leaders of the young nation as she specifically addresses racial, gender, and class injustices that accentuate the radical relationality of all of its members.[2] I also provide brief commentary on Cooper's use of naturalistic imagery, exploring points of convergence between her evolutionary tropes and organic imagery and a vein of thought emanating from the Romantic naturalists. In doing so, I connect her ideas to a trend among nineteenth-century American intellectuals and visionaries, and, more importantly, also emphasize the uniqueness of Cooper's brand of Romanticism. For example, she applied her naturalistic views to myriad cultural settings and social topics that very few of her contemporaries seemed interested in developing, often stressing the humanity of African Americans and other marginalized groups in North America at a time when that humanity was questioned or ignored.

Finally, I discuss the extent to which Cooper challenged her contemporaries to begin the quintessential task of envisioning a new model of humanity. While Cooper does not offer a full or systematic philosophical anthropology, her use of processual language indicates her view of a communal ontology for humanity that is revealed in naturalistic imagery. I connect this aspect of her work to later process thinking with the aim of revealing sympathetic reverberations across the centuries. I contend that Cooper's early efforts culminate in views of human life and national progress that reinscribe deep relationality among all men and women; with such an articulation of communal ontology, she resists imported views of superiority and inferiority among humans. While Cooper does not theorize these themes in the exact manner that I do, her Romantic vision certainly anticipates the capacious humanistic view I develop with the concept of sacred humanity. In this respect, her ideas provide a nice entry point to the African American intellectual trajectory that I see contributing to my emerging African American religious naturalism.

One Voice among Many

In "Our Raison d'Être," the provocative preface to *A Voice from the South*, Cooper addresses the harrowing conditions that had faced African Americans since the Civil War, describing what Du Bois would later call the most perplexing question of twentieth-century America; in her words, "The colored man's inheritance and apportionment is still the sombre crux, the perplexing *cul de sac* of the nation,—the dumb skeleton in the closet provoking ceaseless harangues, indeed, but little understood and seldom consulted."[3] The impact of America's racism on its citizens of African descent, Cooper suggests, awaits full analysis and has yet to be resolved because several significant voices have been silent amid national efforts. Cooper's description of multiple voices—some willfully silent, others muffled, yet others painfully silenced—in these prefatory comments functions as a portal for the multifaceted feminist vision that appears throughout various essays in the volume.[4] In this collection of essays and speeches, Cooper's rhetorical use of *voice* and *voices* (in the title, and in the text itself, in reference to the embodied, raced, and gendered author, and to the collective platform of reform for various groups) functions as a reminder to American leaders that the nation (the "one") must fulfill its destiny in enhancing and securing the vital flourishing of all its "various" parts. In "Our Raison d'Être" and throughout the volume, Cooper uses richly textured, nuanced language and figures of speech to advance this particular point, revealing layers of interpretation from diverse perspectives (social, ethical, feminist, philosophic, and so forth).

Cooper's rhetorical skill is first evidenced when she likens the "Silent" South to the figure of the Sphinx, who functioned in ancient mythologies to symbolize knowledge that humans need but that is hidden from them. The Sphinx figures largely in Egyptian and Greek myth, but often in significantly different ways. In Egyptian contexts, the recumbent male Sphinx figures or sculptures symbolized divine kingship, protective power, and stability. These iconic features and qualities of the Sphinx went through a fascinating reversal during the figure's centuries-long translation through the Middle East to Greece, as it disappeared and reappeared over the course of approximately eight hundred years, roughly from the twelfth through the fourth centuries B.C.E. The male Sphinx of the Egyptians, who transmits the oracles of the gods in the Oedipus myth and Greek mythology, resurfaces as an upright, winged female figure, at once sensual (breasted and svelte) and threatening. Here, rather than guarding gates, the Sphinx is a threatening being who distracts from the danger already within them. In the trajectory of Western thought derived from the Greek heritage, the Sphinx poses riddles learned from oracles. The Sphinx and her messages are associated with diversion, obfuscation, and almost impossible inscrutability instead of transmission, translation, and interpretation. Sphinxes block us and ask us, as did Socrates, to know ourselves—as in the classic riddle, "What walks on four legs in the morning, two legs at noon, and three at close of day?" to which the answer is, "A human being."[5]

I trace this complex lineage to suggest that although Cooper was cashing in on the Sphinx's semiotic value among the educated, enlightened readers of her generation, she was using its cultural currency in an unprecedented, revolutionary manner. During the nineteenth century, the Sphinx was an icon attractive to writers in the young American nation. These intellectuals and idealistic visionaries associated the Sphinx with knowledge and with the ancient cultures of Greece, Rome, and Egypt.[6] Cooper's evocation of the Sphinx, however, raises important gender and racial implications for the nation. Within the American South, she asserts, there are muffled voices—those of black men—and silent voices—those of black women—belonging to those whose lives are most fully affected by the "problem" facing the nation. In juxtaposing the stubborn, enigmatic silence of the South with the imposed silence of black women, Cooper simultaneously addresses the legacy of racism and misogyny bequeathed by Southern slavery and imbues the ancient symbol of the Sphinx with multivocality. She also reinscribes the (Greek) femininity of the Sphinx; however, rather than posing riddles and creating distraction, the vital and crucial voice(s) of black women will help solve what "is often conceded to be a 'puzzling' case" (iii).

Using the trope of the great lawsuit to address the travesty of justice associated with slavery and its aftermath, Cooper reveals the blindness of those advocating either for or against the rights of African Americans (and, by implication, essentially determining their humanity), pointing out that they have overlooked one crucial witness. In a subtle, ingenious gesture, she points beyond the "silent" Sphinx (the white South) to the voice of the southern black woman: "The 'other side' has not been represented by one who 'lives there.' And not many can more sensibly realize and more accurately tell the weight and the fret of the 'long dull pain' than the open-eyed but hitherto voiceless Black Woman of America" (ii). Assuming that America is conscientiously committed to fairness and will be accepting of clear evidence presented to it, Cooper posits a commonsense approach to truth and a perspectivism that justifies the inclusion of black women's perspectives and experiences. Furthermore, in giving voice to a generation of women whose humanity had been compromised, and whose wisdom and self-determination had been suppressed too long by a legacy of forced labor and exploitation, Cooper metes out indispensable knowledge for securing nineteenth-century American progress. Forty years before Simone de Beauvoir unmasked the problematic masculinist bias in Sartre's ontological notion of *pour-soi-en-soi* and in his concept of human freedom, Cooper had begun applying gender analysis to various debates regarding the humanity of blacks amid efforts to secure and justify their freedom and civil rights.

The One and All: Cooper's Vision of America as an Unfolding, Relational Whole

Within the context of addressing America's educational, moral, and spiritual progress, Cooper believed that the women's movement of her age embodied a universalism that united all efforts for human fulfillment (121–22). Accordingly, for Cooper, woman's voice was the paradigmatic voice of the age, speaking for all marginalized and oppressed groups in America; she also persuasively argued that the least voice among all women's voices (that of the black southern woman) would emerge as a vital factor in securing the hopes, dreams, and destiny of the young nation. In various essays in the volume, Cooper's black southern female voice proclaims a promising future for America that would help establish its honor in the world's eyes: America as a potent, vital force in the world, a place where liberty, justice, freedom from oppressive forces, and other democratic principles would flourish on behalf of all its denizens, establishing and honoring their full humanity.

Cooper's hopes and assumptions were grounded in a conception of America as an unfolding cultural sphere where "regenerating" and "vitalizing" forces were at work—a "relational whole" advancing in growth and perfection for all its constituents (11, 18, 21, 26, 29).[7] She persistently uses

evolutionary, dynamic imagery befitting natural processes to portray national transformation and promise. For example, in "Has America a Race
Problem; If So, How Can It Best Be Solved?" Cooper speaks prophetically
of a point in the future when the evolution of America will be evident, of
the ushering in of an unprecedented age when the voice (or interest) of
each and all will be heard and acknowledged (166). She also sketches a view
of America as a vital entity whose maturation is crucial for the unfolding of
a divine will in history. She employs a naturalistic image to convey American civilization presenting a climactic historical moment, describing it as
"a bright consummate flower unfolding *charity toward all and malice toward
none*" (ibid; Cooper's emphasis). For Cooper, a robust America would be
one that persistently sought to provide the necessary conditions in which
all forms of humanity could flourish; it would be the site where the flow-
ering of democratic principles would help alleviate the social problems
associated with systematic discriminatory practices and the corruptions
derived from political tyranny, religious bigotry, and intellectual intoler-
ance. She states, "And I confess I can pray for no nobler destiny for my
country than that it may be the stage, however far distant in the future,
whereon these ideas and principles shall ultimately mature; and culminat-
ing here at whatever cost of production shall go forth hence to dominate
the world" (168).

   In another essay, "Womanhood: A Vital Element in the Regeneration
and Progress of a Race," Cooper again expresses great faith in the progress
of American civilization, speaking even more specifically of the transformative potential of its religious and moral principles. Noting the vigor
and wealth of America, she writes, "We have not yet reached our ideal in
American civilization. . . . But there can be no doubt that here in America
is the arena in which the next triumph of civilization is to be won, and here
too we find promise abundant and possibilities infinite" (12). Cooper read
widely and often cites influential figures to advance her argument; *A Voice
from the South* abounds with references to figures ranging from Sappho
through Shakespeare, William Wordsworth, Ralph Waldo Emerson, and
George Eliot to Frances Watkins Harper and Charlotte Fortin Grimke.
As a result, her lexicon reflects a Euro-American trajectory of progress
and idealism, and she often advances these themes by appealing to views of
human nature that reflected the optimism of the age. For example, she includes insights from the luminous figure of Madame de Staël (1766–1817),
the French-Swiss author and early champion of women's rights often associated with French literary history and the Romantic movement in the
eighteenth and nineteenth centuries.[8] Cooper advanced de Staël's notion

that human happiness "consists not in perfections attained, but in a sense of progress, the result of our own endeavor under conspiring circumstances *toward* a goal which continually advances and broadens and deepens till it is swallowed up in the Infinite" (12).

Cooper was not a Pollyanna, however; she speaks of potential, not actuality. She simultaneously lauds the glory and emergence of the young nation upon the world's stage, and decries its inability to concretize such noble values and ideals in its historical treatment of some of its members. In short, for Cooper, if any part is held back, then the whole is diminished. With this general outlook, Cooper insists that unless, and until, black women and men (and other marginalized groups) can prosper and participate fully in the rich unfolding of America, the nation will not actualize itself. She consistently reminds the country that in its striving for wholeness and unity, it should measure national success in terms of how well each part recognizes its interdependence within a matrix of mutually enriching forces. In other words, Cooper envisions America as a relational whole in which the destinies of the one and the all are inextricably tied together. She develops a feminist discourse teeming with organic metaphors that reveal crucial interconnectedness among the various parts, offering examples from history, logical argumentation, and basic common sense to advance her theme of a relational whole.

Cooper sometimes expresses this keen sense of the interconnectedness of human life in the pious aspects of her feminist discourse. Her speech "Womanhood: A Vital Element in the Regeneration and Progress of a Race" was originally delivered to the exclusively black male clergy of the Protestant Episcopal Church in Washington, D.C. in 1886. Cooper exhorted the audience to do good work and to help those who were most vulnerable to the vicissitudes of slavery and its aftermath, those who were seen as the least part of the whole: that is, poor southern black women. She believed that those who have material prosperity must continue a process of giving back—helping the least because they, too, are essential to the whole. In this speech as in other writings, Cooper uses natural imagery to accentuate her point: "Not even the senseless vegetable is content to be a mere reservoir. Receiving without giving is an anomaly in nature. Nature's cells are all little workshops for manufacturing sunbeams, the product to be *given out* to earth's inhabitants in warmth, energy, thought, action" (46; Cooper's emphasis).

Furthermore, in reiterating the vital role of women in securing national and cultural progress, a common theme among nineteenth-century feminists, Cooper reminds her black male contemporaries that racial regeneration and progress were doomed unless black women were provided with the conditions necessary to their flourishing. The veracity of this claim was so evident to Cooper that again using naturalistic imagery to underscore her point, she asks her contemporaries, "'Women's influence on social progress'—who in Christendom doubts or questions it? One may as well be called on to prove that the sun is the source of light and heat and energy to this many-sided little world" (24). In Sphinx-like fashion, Cooper articulates to her black male contemporaries a necessary truth when addressing racial progress: it was inextricably connected to improving the lives of impoverished black women; without such improvement in the lives of individual black women, community and national advancement could not be achieved. For Cooper, national values and customs derived from ill-conceived racial, gender, and social class differentiations kept both individuals and groups from flourishing and achieving their fullest human potential. As in other cases, she appeals to natural imagery to make essential connections between the flourishing of impoverished black women and the increase in racial and national prosperity.

> Real progress is growth. It must begin in the seed. Then "first the blade, then the ear, after that the full corn in the ear." There is something to encourage and inspire us in the advancement of individuals since their emancipation from slavery. It at least proves that there is nothing irretrievably wrong in the shape of the black man's skull, and that under given circumstances his development, downward or upward, will be similar to that of other average human beings. (26)

Various feminist scholars have assessed Cooper's characterization of impoverished black women, some speaking of a class bias in her tone, and others of her presumption in claiming to speak for all black southern women.[9] While the former critique may be viable to some extent, and the latter may be a concern for those interested in the problem of authorial representation, both critiques must be measured against the overall (albeit subtle) Romantic vision that I think Cooper was advancing in these essays. In other words, Cooper's cultural criticisms rested on the cosmological notion that interconnectedness is one of the basic features of life, and that all entities are members of one another. Her ultimate vision of reform rested on a collective, communal ontology that challenged the notion of superiority based on material wealth and other incidents that she would call arbitrary (125). Moreover, Cooper's perceived personal biases may also reflect the historical exigencies and forces that can sometimes constrain and limit an individual's abstract conceptualizations. Finally, contemporary readers should note that

Cooper's expressions of charity toward poor southern black women often focused attention on dire material conditions and structural forces that contributed to certain members of the nation remaining weak, impoverished, and unable to speak for themselves.

Another important component of Cooper's general theme of the relational whole is the idea that black growth, creativity, and potential productivity were impeded by atomistic conceptualizations of society and stifled by forces that opposed natural life's inherent desire to thrive. When speaking of the racial struggle in "The Status of Woman in America," Cooper uses more natural metaphors—this time to emphasize the necessity of developing black creativity and securing emancipation from stifling and stagnant forces that thwart self-actualization. In one instance, she cites the words of an unidentified European writer who observes, "Except the Sclavonic, the Negro is the only original and distinctive genius which has yet to come to growth—and the feeling is to cherish and develop it" (144). For Cooper, one of the greatest gifts that America could offer itself was to both promote and maintain the proper conditions whereby its proud, young, gifted black citizens could fulfill themselves and facilitate communal and national growth and productivity, as echoed in such declarations as "Aha, I can rival that! I can aspire to that" (144). In associating *genius* with *blackness*, Cooper wanted to show her peers that the cultivation of black life and its vital forces cohered both with the natural order of things, and with national and universal transformation.[10] Furthermore, in this context, Cooper was advocating a vital construction of African Americans' full, complex humanity, which had been consistently erased by stereotypes of blacks as abundant, resourceful bodies suited only for material labor.

Cooper advances her vision using the trope of nature as a historicizing mirror that illustrates the notion of America as a relational whole, or as a cultural sphere producing the necessary, crucial growth of all Americans, not just a chosen few (117, 176, 177). When speaking out against various forms of oppression and cultural imperialism, Cooper argues that such developments are not in keeping with nature's design: "Now I need not say that peace produced by suppression is neither natural nor desirable. Despotism is not one of the ideas that man has copied from nature" (150). Cooper's understanding of historical progress necessitated the interaction of vital forces contending fairly with one another. In her worldview, what was so deplorable about any form of discrimination was its systemic silencing and tyrannical imposition upon natural forces and vital processes that inherently desired to fulfill themselves. She again emphasized nature's role in helping us to see such truths: "All through God's universe we see eternal harmony and symmetry as the unvarying result of the equilibrium of opposing forces. Fair play in an equal fight is the law written in Nature's book. And the solitary bully with his foot on the breast of his last antagonist has no warrant in any fact of God" (150).

An interesting aspect of Cooper's theoretical worldview is that in it some forms of conflict are inevitable among the individual parts, because each has its own unique persuasion and will to be, which, ideally, contributes to the whole. To advance her views, Cooper provides examples from natural processes whose movements and interactions with one another offer truths that are beneficial and crucial to human growth and well-being. She asserts:

> The beautiful curves described by planets and suns in their courses are the resultant of conflicting forces. Could the centrifugal force for one instant triumph, or should the centripetal grow weary and give up the struggle, immeasurable disaster would ensue—earth, moon, sun would go spinning off at a tangent or must fall helplessly into its master sphere. . . . A proper equilibrium between a most inflammable explosive and the supporter of combustion, gives us water, the bland fluid that we cannot dispense with. Nay, the very air we breathe, which seems so calm, so peaceful, is rendered innocuous only by the constant conflict of opposing gases. Were the fiery, never-resting, all-corroding oxygen to gain the mastery we should be burnt to cinders in a trice. With the sluggish, inert nitrogen triumphant, we should die of inanition.
> (150–51)

The general lesson found here is that a proper, structural relationship exists between elements of nature such that they fit together harmoniously as necessary parts of the whole. Moreover, Cooper argues, nature's movements are epitomized in the human realm when people (functioning either as nations or as individuals) constantly strive to actualize themselves on an even playing ground in the absence of such socially constructed disturbances as despotism, race tyranny, suppression, and various forms of cultural domination.

In addressing America's capacity to deal with its race problem by providing the necessary conditions for human freedom, Cooper's cosmological vision occasionally evokes a teleological view of a divine will acting in history. By the same token, she also argues for a type of participatory citizenship in which each part has a crucial role amid the natural conflicts that arise from the proximity of differences. In securing democratic ideals, one law holds fast: "[I]n sociology as in the world of matter, *that equilib-*

rium, not repression among conflicting forces is the condition of natural harmony, of permanent progress, and of universal freedom" (160; Cooper's emphasis). To underscore her point, Cooper inserts an important historiographical insight: the ideals associated with human freedom that she celebrates in the young nation were born and shaped in a modern European context that has experienced several centuries of racial, cultural, and ethnic diversity amid conflictual engagement. For Cooper, however, it is the young America of her day that has the potential to become the "consummation of the ideal of human possibilities," and, consequently, the proper arena for the interplay of forces and conflict in which diversity becomes standard (161). In the last analysis, then, for Cooper, the nation's growth will involve inevitable conflict as it evolves toward sustaining a rich, civilized culture of celebrating differences; in this context, healthy, stimulating, and progressive conflict consists of "the co-existence of radically opposing or racially different elements," which can contribute to a peaceful, harmonious way of life only when it is conceived as constituted by differences, and where the general ethos is "the determination to live and let live" (151; 149).

Cooper's Unique Slant on the Romantic Interplay of One and All

Cooper's ingenious use of natural imagery and rhetorical tropes in advancing the theme of America as a relational whole is richly suggestive of a Romantic strain in her work. I detect some intriguing points of convergence between Cooper's belief in the inextricable destiny of each (one) and all (many) and an influential Romantic vision of nature, which was ushered in by William Blake (1757–1827) and other English visionaries who conceived of nature as an organic whole.[11] Targeting the reductionism of Newton that ensued from the mechanistic Cartesian paradigm, and using the macro-micro analogy, Blake considered humans to be more than a collection of separate atoms.[12] Blake and other English Romantics also believed that nature should not be divorced from aesthetic values, which were for them just as real (or even more real) than the abstractions of science. Accordingly, these figures helped to shape a Romantic vision of life that conveyed for human organisms worlds of meaning and love and joyful, responsible engagement with otherness.

Sharing some of Blake's concerns, various German Romantic poets and philosophers revived the Aristotelian tradition and concentrated on the nature of organic form as they faced a modern crisis of consciousness produced by reductionist epistemologies. Johann Wolfgang von Goethe (1749–1832), a central figure in this movement, constructed a natural philosophy aimed at rescuing the study of nature from militant scientific reductionism. In his scientific philosophy, Goethe used the term *morphology*, which often described biological form from a dynamic, developmental point of view. Admiring nature's "moving order" (*bewegliche Ordnung*), Goethe conceived of form as a pattern of relationships within an organized whole—a conception that is now in vogue in contemporary systems thinking. He also believed that each creature is a patterned gradation (*Schattierung*) of one great harmonious whole.[13] Furthermore, Goethe rejected the mechanistic views maintained by the science of his time, denying the superiority of rationality as the sole guide to the interpretation of reality. Knowledge, for him, had a perspectival quality that expands the truth of natural observation to a contextual grounding that is irreducible. Such quality is eloquently expressed in the following poetic verses:

> You must, when contemplating nature,
> Attend to this, in each and every feature:
> There's nought outside and nought within,
> For she is inside out and outside in.
> Thus will you grasp, with no delay,
> The holy secret, clear as day.
>
> Joy in true semblance take, in any
> Earnest play:
> No living thing is One, I say,
> But always Many.[14]

It is difficult to know for certain whether Cooper read Goethe directly or studied him extensively when writing her essays. What seems apparent is that her feminist appraisal of the vital and inextricable intersections of America's constitutive parts parallels, in very subtle and often compelling ways, insights supremely expressed in Goethe's poetic and philosophic reflections on nature. In Cooper's nineteenth-century feminist discourse, however, the general abstract notion of one and all that Goethe and other European and American visionaries employed becomes concretized, politicized, and historicized along race and gender lines. It is this attention to racial and gender issues that illuminates the uniqueness at that time of Cooper's Romanticism-infused discourse.

While applauding the wonders of the nascent and notoriously bucolic nation, Cooper criticizes America for its attempted suppression of a vital element of its own being: African American women and men. She states, "We are the heirs of a past which was not our fathers' moulding. 'Every man the arbiter of his own destiny' was not true for the American Negro of the past: and it is no fault of his that he finds himself to-day the inheritor of a manhood and womanhood impoverished and debased by two centuries and more of compression and degradation" (28). Believing that racial and gender discriminatory practices in the nation had reduced corporeal, relational, vital African Americans to pure objects of knowledge, Cooper thus utters oracles becoming of the Sphinx. Furthermore, when advocating for the advanced education of all women, Cooper questions the myopic views of black male leaders whose impoverished constructions of masculinity and femininity considered black women's intellectual development both inessential and frivolous amid graver social issues (75). Just as her black counterparts argued that a free black (fully human) race was essential to the progress of the nation, so Cooper, too, reminded all of her comrades that an educated and enlightened womanhood was a vital key to the success of the country. She employed wonderful metaphors, such as that of the body and its members, to emphasize this perspective: "The world has had to limp along with the wobbling gait and one-sided hesitancy of a man with one eye. Suddenly the bandage is removed and the whole body is filled with light. It sees a circle where before it saw a segment. The darkened eye restored, every member rejoices with it" (122–23).

Cooper's metaphor works on two levels. It first points to a metaphysical truth involving the coordination of microcosm and macrocosm—the part and the whole are linked to one another in a seamless web of process or becoming. As each member aspires to become a vital participant in the whole, it simultaneously fulfills itself and completes the whole. Second, Cooper's image evokes a savvy feminist political consciousness wary of an atomistic worldview that pits particular groups (for example, black men versus white women, women versus Indians, black women versus white women) against one another in their efforts to gain the vote and flourish. Rejecting an isolationist approach to reform in America, she declares, "It is not the intelligent woman vs. the ignorant woman; nor the white woman vs. the black, the brown, and the red,—it is not even the cause of woman vs. man. Nay, 'tis woman's strongest vindication for speaking that *the world needs to hear her voice*. It would be subversive of every human interest that the cry of one-half the human family be stifled" (121; Cooper's emphasis). The harsh critiques Cooper directs toward misguided American norms and values were shaped by her awareness that the nation had lost its sense of itself as a relational whole, so to speak—a purportedly enlightened, robust Western nation was in actuality a ghastly, crippling body deceptively blind to the needs of its most vulnerable, yet vital, members.

In challenging a popular American sentiment that spoke of human progress and advancement while various groups suffered from unjust social stigma and dehumanizing cultural practices, Cooper provided a unique slant on the theme of the inextricable connection of one and all—a whiff of American Romanticism that is also evident in Emerson, Whitman, and other influential figures.[15] In specific essays, Cooper appears particularly receptive to the insights of Emerson, a key figure among the Concord intellectuals who would later call themselves the Transcendentalists. Rejecting the staid, stifling Victorian sensibilities of nineteenth-century America, Emerson and other Transcendentalists sought to introduce a revolutionary new populism into the already hierarchical American democratic system. Emerson particularly confronted the existing intellectual elite, most conspicuously represented by the Harvard community, as he sought to expand America's principles of justice. Cooper often cites Emerson's proto-feminist sentiments and similar expressions articulated by other influential thinkers of the day in order to raise gender awareness (12–13). She also includes Emerson's perspectives on the intricacies and movements of nature when advancing her theme of one and all (47, 66).

Cooper's references to Emerson are significant because he and the other New England Transcendentalists extensively discussed and debated Goethe; several of them translated Goethe's works into English.[16] Emerson also owned the complete 55-volume edition of Goethe's works published by J. G. Cotta in Stuttgart (1827–1833), and due, in part, to Emerson's influence in American letters and philosophy in the nineteenth century, crucial Goethean themes became established on American soil.[17] A key passage from Emerson's essay "The Over-Soul" conveys one of the most direct and strongest examples of American Romanticism, specifically expanding the Goethean theme of one and all:

> We live in succession, in division, in parts, in particles. Meantime within man is the soul of the whole; the wise silence; the universal beauty, to which every part and particle is equally related; the eternal ONE. And this deep power in which we exist, and whose beatitude is all accessible to us, is not only self-sufficing and perfect in every hour, but the act of seeing and the thing seen, the seer and the spectacle, the subject and the object, are one. We see the world piece by piece, as the sun, the moon, the animal, the tree; but the whole, of which these are the shining parts, is the soul.[18]

Cooper's referencing of Emerson, de Staël, and other radical thinkers from Europe and America shows the extent to which she strategically appropriated the knowledge of her era to pursue a trajectory of thought that was not as fully advanced by either her white peers or her black male counterparts. Her citation of these iconic white writers also suggest Cooper's astuteness with regard to the realities facing marginalized writers, especially those addressing topics that the majority of readers would consider inessential or trivial. Among black and female writers, there was also a sobering awareness of the considerable, tangible difficulties they faced in trying to get their work published. Cooper's precarious (and unique) status as a black woman author of this time cannot be overemphasized. As Vivian May persuasively argues, Cooper was trying to negotiate at least two worlds at once in her published texts and in her life: "an ideal world in which her personhood would not be questioned and, simultaneously, lived reality in which she had to contest daily the weight of being perceived and treated as 'other.'" [19] Her theories were not merely abstract ideas; they emerged out of her embodied experiences as a black woman, scholar, educator, author, and activist in the early part of the twentieth century whose full humanity was questioned. This lived experience of her black humanity makes Cooper's view of problematic racial, gender, and class distinctions as distortions of the relational whole even more compelling and forceful. Her feminist analysis was unflinching in its demand for egalitarian principles and its advocacy of a capacious vision of humanity's flourishing.

One of the strongest expressions of Cooper's one-and-all vision is found in her essay titled "The Indian versus the Woman," in which Cooper makes crucial connections between various forms of prejudice and argues essentially that "the philosophic mind sees that its own 'rights' are the rights of humanity" (118). In her own way, Cooper points to the ever-looming presence of what Michel Foucault would later identify as subjugated voices, or disruptions to the current episteme. In "The Higher Education of Women," she confronts the historical amnesia and imperialism of Western European writers who imposed a distorted historical consciousness on the current Western age in seeing it as the supreme achievement of past eras, portraying Western culture as triumphantly surpassing other cultures. One target of Cooper's critique is Percival Lowell's outlook in *Soul of the Far East* (1888), in which he argues, among other things, that "'As for Far Orientals, they are not of those who will survive. . . . If these people continue in their old course, their early career is closed. Just as surely as morning passes into afternoon, so surely are these races of the Far East, if unchanged, destined to disappear before the advancing nations of the West'" (52). In these quoted words of Lowell, Cooper detects the same triumphalist and xenophobic spirit that had been at work in America's justification of slavery and that was still evident in its treatment of African Americans. She thus responds, in a spirited manner: "A spectacle to make the gods laugh, truly, to see the scion of an upstart race by one sweep of his generalizing pen consigning to annihilation one-third of the inhabitants of the globe—a people whose civilization was hoary headed before the partner elements that begot his race had advanced beyond nebulosity" (ibid.). Here Cooper is also unmasking and investigating the cultural imperialism lurking in the dominant ideological assumptions of Western visionaries who despised what they perceived as the weaknesses of people of Asian and African descent, whom they viewed as less evolved than themselves.[20]

In "Woman versus the Indian," Cooper also offers a scathing attack on southern American culture (which she sometimes symbolized as a powerful white male owner), suggesting that it has provided the germ for the corrupt sensibilities and moral conventions of the country: "Indeed, the Southerner is a magnificent manager of men, a born educator. For two hundred and fifty years he trained to his hand a people whom he made absolutely his own, in body, mind, and sensibility. He so insinuated differences and distinctions among them, that their personal attachment for him was stronger than for their own brethren and fellow sufferers" (101–02). In the same essay, Cooper expresses indignation at the thought shared by many white southern women, namely, that efforts to secure the rights of blacks in society seemed to run against the *natural* order of things. For Cooper, the desire for self-fulfillment expressed by U.S. blacks and other marginalized groups (as well as their efforts to humanize their material existence) were cultural manifestations of a higher truth that must not be deterred. She concludes that such aspirations are universal, that they are strivings after "the one ideal of perfect manhood and womanhood, the one universal longing for development and growth, the one desire for being, and being better, the one yearning, aspiring, outreaching, in all heartthrobs of humanity in whatever race or clime" (113).

With her unique Romantic strain, Cooper made crucial connections between patterns of growth and development within human life and those found in the realm of nature. A key passage found in "One Phase of American Literature" has Cooper addressing the problems encountered when one individual, culture, or race purports to dominate and represent another in ways that are not representative of the other's vitality and potential growth. She uses the trope of nature to help illustrate the processes of growth, development, and evolution of America's constitutive parts that must participate in the dynamic, organic, relational whole. In this case, Cooper reinscribes nature's wisdom by depicting the wrong type of "cultivation" that occurs when humans do not heed nature's insights about the relational whole:

> Nature's language is not writ in cipher. Her notes are always simple and sensuous, and the very meanest recesses and commonest byways are fairly deafening with her sermons and songs. It is only when we ourselves are out of tune through our pretentiousness and self-sufficiency, or we are blinded and rendered insensate by reason of our foreign and unnatural "cultivation" that we miss her meanings and inadequately construe her multiform lessons. (177–78)

This passage from Cooper parallels Goethe's concern to demonstrate the connection between human life and that of the rest of nature. Goethe believed nature held a pervasive pattern of process, of formation and transformation, which was accessible to the human observer by way of a certain type of introspection and observation. [21] Regarding growth as essentially self-production, Goethe assumed that human life had essentially the same pattern of development that one could trace in the growth of plants—although the human case is more complex and harder to observe. In this context, he spoke repeatedly of the *Bildung* (or the development and cultivation) of plants. [22] Goethe's use of the term *Bildung* was part of an important trend among German intellectuals and artists who in the late eighteenth century debated its specific meaning and manifestation. [23] Goethe defined his idea of *Bildung* with his own concepts of metamorphosis and morphology as a natural, organic process of maturation as well as a pedagogic principle leading to an overall harmonic wholeness. This same term was also operative in Wilhelm von Humboldt's pedagogical theory and practice, in which the aim of education was the development, or cultivation, of the human individual, and in subsequent generations *Bildung* became an influential term in Western culture. [24]

As noted earlier, Emerson and other nineteenth-century writers were very receptive to Goethean ideas, helping to transport them onto American soil. They especially appreciated and supported Goethe's notion of *Bildung*, or the complete and harmonious development of the individual, as it enriched and contributed to their understanding of self-culture. It is not surprising, therefore, to see Cooper, the quintessential educator and visionary intellectual, sharing these perspectives. She constantly encouraged black women and men to seek self-fulfillment and self-actualization, urging them to secure their rights and participate in "a great and international movement characteristic of this age and country, a movement based on the inherent right of every soul to its highest development" (108). Behind this view of self-determination is Cooper's philosophic sense that the vital processual nature of human life itself supersedes what has been typically (and ignorantly) taken to be descriptive of black life, in particular, and of American life in general. In her address to the black male church leaders, Cooper asserts, "And here let me say parenthetically that our satisfaction in American institutions rests not on the fruition we now enjoy, but springs rather from the possibilities and promise that are inherent in the system, though as yet, perhaps, far in the future" (11–12).

Cooper's thought was provocative in its dismantling of who or what nineteenth-century Americans thought they were—or had been conceived to be by cultural spin doctors bogged down by distorted ontological *gravitas*. She encouraged black women and men to move from passivity and stupor to action and self-direction, exhorting them to counter whites' distortions imposed from outside, and to resist self-effacing condemnations buried within themselves. Accordingly, she employed a naturalistic theme that emphasized the vital movement from objectivity to subjectivity, and from being dehumanized to enacting one's humanity. Citing Emerson again, Cooper declares: "We want the will which advances and dictates [acts]. Nature has made up her mind that what cannot defend itself, shall not be defended. Complaining never so loud and with never so much reason, is of no use. What cannot stand must fall" (47). There is a sense of self-determination and a celebration of self-actualization in Cooper's reasoning that cannot be denied, and it is this aspect of her thought that reverberates most vividly as Romantic naturalism. In her view, individual will and self-actualization within the entity itself emphasizes a personal, intuitive, and personalized form of expression and polity of natural processes.

Intimations of Sacred Humanity in Cooper's Worldview

Although Cooper never fully develops a systematic philosophical anthropology in the collection of essays, she does provide examples that characterize humans as evolving, perfecting, and maturing processes. In the last essay in *A Voice from the South*, "The Gain from a Belief," for example, Cooper employs processual imagery to describe human life while challenging the skepticism and positivism of various European philosophers who saw human beings as nothing more than conglomerations of cells best explained by scientific empiricism. Negating such gross reductionism, she sketches a much loftier view of humanity's participation in a "sublime conception of life as the seed-time of character for the growing of a congenial inner-self to be forever a constant presence" (295). With this sense of an evolving, dynamic quality to human life, Cooper tries to dismantle problematic constructions of the human within the dominant desacralized cosmologies constructed by racist and sexist dogmatists. In this context, Cooper also provides an interesting perspective on faith. Rejecting dominant views of faith as either proper (or orthodox) interpretations or the establishment of doctrinal certainties, Cooper endorses a conception of faith as the enactment of one's truth through one's actions. Specifically, faith is born of a pragmatism that both perceives and recognizes in human beings the capacity to perfect and expand themselves. She sees this exercise of faith in the historical figure of Jesus, whom she describes as following:

> Jesus *believed* in the infinite possibilities of an individual soul. His faith was . . . an optimistic vision of the human aptitude for endless expansion and perfectibility. This truth to him placed a sublime valuation on each individual sentiency. . . . He could not lay hold of this truth and allow his own benevolence to be narrowed and distorted by the trickeries of circumstance or the colorings of prejudice. (298)

Cooper's view of human life was inextricably tied to her awareness of its natural unfolding and of its emergence from a greater matrix of natural forces that were life-affirming for all, not just for a few. She thematizes these truths as she addresses "negrophobia" in another essay entitled "What Are We Worth?" For Cooper, the term represents the rampant cultural blindness that failed to grasp and appreciate the true worth of black humans. Undaunted, however, she envisions a future where the essential worth of black humanity and its potential contributions to the world of human culture will be recognized:

> As sure as time *is—these mists will clear away*. And the world—our world, will surely and unerringly see us as we are. Our only care need be the intrinsic worth of our contributions. . . . [I]f we contribute a positive value in those things the world prizes, no amount of negrophobia can ultimately prevent its recognition. And our great "problem" after all is to be solved not by brooding over it, and orating about it, but by *living into it*. (284–85; Cooper's emphases)

Bearing in mind my concept of sacred humanity, Cooper's use of the term *negrophobia* evokes an impoverished view of humanity that fails to see each human life as a center of value. There is another respect in which her view of humanity and my concept of sacred humanity converge. Cooper believed this future could unfold only when human culture, informed by the insights offered by evolutionary imagery, both enhanced and built on what was intrinsically vital to human life: its emergence based on its past. Within the context of America's racial bigotry, which she refers to as "mists" of misunderstanding that have resulted in distorted relations with one another, she advocated for the cultivation of human life through education. As an consummate educator, Cooper believed that the material, relational human being was a dynamic, malleable entity capable of trans-formative growth if only we provided the proper conditions and forms of cultivation for its maturation: "It is labor, development, training, careful patient, diligent toil that must span the gulf between this vegetating life germ (now worth nothing but toil and care and trouble, and living purely at the expense of another)—and that future consummation in which 'the elements are so mixed that Nature can stand up and say to all the world, "This is a man"'" (244). In keeping with her capacious worldview, Cooper believed an evolved humanity necessitated the elimination of racial bigotry as well as other forms of human wreckage in which any manifestation of full humanity was denied its potential. Throughout the volume, Cooper asks her readers—sometimes with righteous indignation, at other times with the most brilliant wit—to help re-envision the human as an important finite realm (or, perhaps, as constituting a unique value-laden matrix) of potentiality within the unfolding of infinite cosmic possibilities (244, 258, 297). With these views of humanity, Cooper adamantly targeted a crass materialism that she ultimately rejected on religious terms: "Life must be something more than dilettante speculation. And religion (ought to be if it isn't) a great deal more than mere gratification of the instinct for worship linked with the straight-teaching of irreproachable credos. Religion must be *life made true*, and life is action, growth, development—begun now and ending never" (299).

Cooper on Nature's Truths and Our Radical Relationality: Future Prospects

Cooper's feminist vision demanded radical and structural changes in all spheres of American society: the work force, political and educational are-nas, familial and social structures, and cultural activities. In all these re-spects, her critiques extended the Goethean-infused interplay of the one and the many, evoking a processual view of life that dates back to Aristotle,[25] in which experience, feeling, power, and potentiality are the key catego-ries that structure the nation's growth as an organic, wholistic entity. For Cooper, a deeply transformed America would be clearly evident in how well its educational, social, artistic, and political structures provided the conditions for African Americans and other oppressed groups to actualize and perfect themselves. In demanding this level of transformation for America, Cooper's unique brand of Romantic humanism reverberates with the poignant liberationist theme of black religiosity. Moreover, there is, for me, the allure of Cooper's method of establishing the dignity and value of blacks' humanity through the use of naturalistic imagery. In short, Cooper's propensity to seek and outline truths embedded in nature, and her sustained focus on (human) nature's movements, albeit expressed in her nineteenth-century Romantic language, signal a critical stage, or perhaps the germination, of the trajectory of thought that I associate with the emergence of an African American religious naturalism. A cluster of ideas focusing on nature's movements, chief of which is the observation that a nexus of relations constitutes nature, artfully shapes this perspective. Indeed, while emphasizing the key metaphor of relationality to describe the fundamental truth of human life, Cooper foreshadows a particular feature of my naturalistic orientation that is aligned with contemporary process thought. After providing a brief overview of process thought, I will indicate the extent to which her ideas anticipate this orientation.

Modern process thought emerged in the early twentieth century, although its antecedents reach as far back as some pre-Socratic philosophies. Its development also owes as much to Anne Conway and the vitalists of the seventeenth century as it does to such later theorists as Charles Bergson, Alfred N. Whitehead, Francis H. Bradley, and Charles S. Peirce.[26] In some form or another, all of these figures challenged the primacy of mechanistic and deterministic interpretations of causality as adequate or full explanations of natural phenomena. Contemporary process thought remains a confluence of philosophic insights engaged in dismantling the scientific optimism that has escalated over time into a secular form of apocalyptic fulfillment. Process thought diametrically opposes the general view that subordinates processes to substantial things, or denies processes altogether.

Process thought focuses principally on change and temporality: becoming, not being, is the central metaphor for understanding reality, and contingency, emergence, and creativity are essential elements that take precedence over determinism and the static. Process thought encourages us to take very seriously the actuality of change; accordingly, nothing is constant, everything is in flux. This idea resonates with an early observation of Henri Bergson, who in 1911 suggested that "reality appears as a ceaseless upspringing of something new, which has no sooner arisen to make the present than it has already fallen back into the past."[27] Adherents of process thought make the extraordinary claim that to be actual is to be a process. Rejecting the dominant substance ontology, which posits reality as material substance, static and nonexperiencing, process meta-physicians often characterize reality as processual, dynamic, and capable of experience. Processes have an objective nature (that is, processes can be experienced by subjects), a subjective nature (processes can experience, are partly self-determining, and can enter into relation with other processes), and a temporal nature (processes happen through time, or, perhaps, de-fine time).

In the early twentieth century, Alfred N. Whitehead offered a remark-ably innovative picture of reality in which the basic unit of nature is not static material substance, but rather creative, experiential events, or actual occasions of experience. In his classic cosmological work, *Process and Real-ity*, Whitehead posits the building blocks of reality as "actual occasions" or processual units, with human experience showing the most supreme exem-plification of these living units of elemental experience.[28] In the language of Whitehead, complex objects are societies, or a nexus, of actual occasions that endure cooperatively. Complex objects are no mere aggregates, but possess a defining unity; this appearance of enduring material substance is actually a result of the stable patterns established by sequential processes. Process philosophers justify all of these claims on the existential grounds that we can only truly understand the units comprising the physical world by analogy with our own experience that we know from within. Experience shapes the very process of becoming that is enjoyed by all actual entities.

Process thought acknowledges a new sort of relationship between expe-rience and consciousness. All actual entities, and not just conscious beings, enjoy experience. Whitehead asserts: "Consciousness presupposes expe-rience, and not experience consciousness."[29] Furthermore, as Whitehead notes, consciousness is primarily a high-level form of experience that be-longs to such high-grade organisms as human beings. This means that we must look within, see the experiences of our life, and understand that they are not things that happen to us, but rather are the fundamental elements of the real that comprise us. We are our experiences and we change with-out ceasing.

In a Whiteheadian processual framework, all entities have subjectivity and responsiveness, and there is a dynamic relationship between individual organisms. Each occurrence in turn exerts influence, which enters into the becoming of other occurrences. The technical Whiteheadian term *internal relations* helps us to make sense of these activities.[30] These basic unit-events of the world are not vacuous, but rather possess a subjective nature that allows them attributes that might be called feeling, memory, and creativity. Every event, while influenced by the past through a process Whitehead calls *prehension*, exercises some amount of self-determination or self-creation.[31] Every event also has some power to exert creative influence on the future. This creative advance into novelty characterizes Whitehead's cosmos.

While she is not a process thinker *per se*, Cooper's understanding of the "one and many" has interesting points of convergence with process thought, leading me to reflect on the theoretical and ethical implications of her naturalistic imagery. Some of Whitehead's conceptual truths regarding nature's movements are indeed discernible in Cooper's vision of the interplay of the one and all. In her portrayal of African Americans, poor black women, and other oppressed groups securing their full humanity, this interplay is expressed most vividly in cultural and ethical terms. In Whitehead, as in Cooper, microcosm and macrocosm are coordinated, linked to one another in a seamless web of process. There is a dialectical tension between individual and world. Each item of existence in nature touches the others and without them would not be what it is.

A clear example of this truth for Cooper is found in "The Higher Education of Women," where she introduces a general complementary principle of gender in her efforts to secure educational advantages for women. Her promotion of gender equality rests on a metaphysical notion of truth in which feminine and masculine qualities constitute the whole (truth) and require one another: "All I claim is that there is a feminine as well as masculine side to truth; that these are related not as inferior and superior, not as better and worse, not as weaker and stronger, but as complements— complements in one necessary and symmetrical whole" (60). Cooper believed that each constructed quality is found in both men and women, and that both are needed to balance the whole person; she further suggests that if one overshadows the other, "a nation or race will degenerate into mere emotionalism on the one hand, or bullyism on the other" (61). On the more practical side, she argues that the nurturing of well-rounded children who are in touch with their masculine and feminine qualities is an effective means for procuring a whole and fulfilled human race. More importantly, Cooper maintains that the world needs the education of women to unlock the feminine side of truth.

In advancing her conception of truth, Cooper quickly notes that while men often seemed more readily drawn to abstraction (a specific quality of "masculinity") and women to empathetic nurturing, (a specific quality of "femininity"), abstract reasoning is not the sole essential property of all men, nor is empathetic nurturing the sole essential property of all women.

Unfortunately, she fails to pursue or clarify this provocative line of thinking, and simply concludes that the consensus is "that one trait is essentially masculine and the other is peculiarly feminine" (61). While Cooper does not provide conceptual clarity in her notion of gender complementary, she assumes its veracity by arguing that the fullness of reality encompasses a feminine force or factor that could radically transform U.S. culture, even the world. The subtle intimation here, of course, is that when the masculinist bias becomes dominant in all spheres of human engagement, there is a lack of wholeness.

With this nebulous gender complementary principle, Cooper attempts to address the chasm between the actual and the ideal, suggesting that a glorified and ennobled human nature is hindered by concrete, historical atrocities. Accordingly, this principle functions in Cooper's feminist discourse to show the inextricable connection between a perfected and emancipated humanity and the specific emancipation of women from patriarchal power structures and values. Attending to the bondage associated with sexist ideologies that constantly threaten to submerge women's agency, Cooper targets patriarchal tactics of adornment and praise that keep women from actualizing their potential as vital selves, especially moral selves. She thus speaks of "a real and special influence of woman. An influence subtle and often involuntary, an influence so intimately interwoven in, so intricately interpenetrated by the masculine influence of the time that it is often difficult to extricate the delicate meshes and analyze and identify the closely clinging fibers" (56).

It is difficult to understand fully Cooper's mystical articulations, but they seem to emerge from her vision of a dynamic sphere of human life—a relational whole—imbued with crucial intersections of force and interactions among individual entities. Cooper's urgent demand that women be educated can be viewed as part of a cosmological urge. In this sense, advocating that women must have the opportunity to learn fully as a vital part of the whole, or to take in all that life has to offer, is comparable to Whitehead's depiction of an organism's feeling and its absorption of the multifarious data of the environment into itself. Here, the pivotal notion of *prehension* in Whitehead's theory comes to mind, as it indicates precisely the point of internal relations between and among actual entities. In *Process and Reality*, Whitehead describes three dimensions of prehension, or three factors associated with it: "(a) the 'subject' which is prehending, namely, the actual entity in which that prehension is a concrete element; (b) the 'datum' which is prehended; (c) the 'subjective form' which is *how* that subject prehends that datum."[32] In Whitehead's three-fold structure of prehension, one imagines a wholistic field of relationality in which the becoming of an actual occasion is informed by a densely teleological sense of the occasion's own ultimate actuality, or its subjective aim.

Whitehead did not extend these important concepts of his philosophy of organism into such spheres as education or culture, specifically as Cooper describes them. However, as Whitehead understood his general cosmological framework, all forms of experience are subsumed within it and could be interpreted by way of it. In *Adventures of Ideas*, Whitehead states:

> In order to discover some of the major categories under which we can classify the infinitely various components of experience, we must appeal to evidence relating to every variety of occasion. Nothing can be omitted, experience drunk and experience sober, experience sleeping and experience waking, experience drowsy and experience wide-awake, experience self-conscious and experience self-forgetful, experience intellectual and experience physical, experience religious and experience sceptical, experience anxious and experience care-free, experience anticipatory and experience retrospective, experience happy and experience grieving, experience dominated by emotion and experience under self-restraint, experience in the light and experience in the dark, experience normal and experience abnormal.[33]

The universal aims underpinning Cooper's demands for higher education for women seems to parallel this Whiteheadian cosmological framework. Furthermore, in her expansive vision, all vital organisms (inclusive of women, blacks, the poor and oppressed) are structured to experience what goes on around them in a way that encompasses a low-grade mode of emotion, consciousness, and purpose. Note, her declaration: "As individuals, we are constantly and inevitably, whether we are conscious of it or not, giving out our real selves into our several little worlds, inexorably adding our own true ray to the flood of starlight, quite independently of our professions and our masquerading" (55). A full humanity in set into play here; an important insight is that Cooper's advocacy for African Americans (especially poor southern black women) cannot be viewed apart from a communal ontology that was anchored in late nineteenth-century Victorian feminist claims for women's influence in the world.

As these examples show, Cooper believed that women's agency in the world would contribute to a richer expansion of truth, or to fuller disclosures of expanding meaning and value in the world. Without the nurturing of this vital (feminine) principle, the whole would remain impoverished, and truth would be incomplete. Thus, according to Cooper's logic, staunch advocacy for women's education was not simply about personal gain for women. As she suggests, "the feminine factor can have its proper effect only through woman's development and education so that she may fitly and intelligently stamp her force on the forces of her day, and add her modicum to the riches of the world's thought" (61). Furthermore, in line with her organic theme of the relational whole, Cooper addresses skeptical and sarcastic responses from men who question women's demands that the feminine force be allowed to influence the world. She replies, "Nature never meant that the ideals and standards of the world should be dwarfing and minimizing ones, and the men should thank us for requiring of them the richest fruits which they can grow" (71).

For Cooper, the capacity of women and men to perfect themselves with knowledge and to perform good, kind actions in the world was crucial for the evolution of civilization. In this respect, she shares Whitehead's view, that "[e]very epoch has its character determined by the way its population re-act to the material events which they encounter. This reaction is determined by their basic beliefs—by their hopes, their fears, their judgments of what is worthwhile."[34] In short, Cooper's feminist outlook essentially desired a world in which mutually enhancing events and dynamic relations among individuals occurred. Her capacious feminism, guided by Romantic idealism, was directed not only toward women, but toward all of humanity. She writes:

> . . . and when the right of the individual is made sacred, when the image of God in human form, whether in marble or in clay, whether in alabaster or in ebony, is consecrated and inviolable, when men have been taught to look beneath the rags and grime, the pomp and pageantry of mere circumstance and have regard unto the celestial kernel uncontaminated at the core,—when race, color, sex, condition, are realized to be the accidents, not the substance of life, and consequently as not obscuring or modifying the inalienable title to life, liberty and pursuit of happiness,—then is mastered the science of politeness, the art of courteous contact, which is . . . the backbone and marrow of religion; then woman's lesson is taught and woman's cause is won. (124–25)

Thus, while Cooper often unmasked the racist sentiments of white reformers, and especially critiqued the blindness of southern white women, she nonetheless commended the women's movement of her day for its universal scope and aim, seeing it ideally as a compassionate phenomenon which, if allowed to achieve its goal, would generate a more humane and free society. Her gender critique was also at the heart of her felt religios-

ity, which aimed for a habit of the heart and mind that cultivates self-love
in conjunction with love of others—an undeniably crucial aspect of processual nature as desirous of fulfillment. Expressed in more poetic terms,
Cooper anticipated sacred humanity in vital movements toward good and
right relations with others. She declares:

> For women's cause is the cause of the weak; and when all the weak
> shall have received their due consideration, then woman will have her
> "rights," and the Indian will have his rights, and the Negro will have
> his rights, and all the strong will have learned at last to deal justly, to
> love mercy, and to walk humbly; and our fair land will have been taught
> the secret of universal courtesy which is after all nothing but the art,
> the science, and the religion of regarding one's neighbor as one's self,
> and to do for him as we would, were conditions swapped, that he do for
> us. (117)

Moreover, as noted earlier, Cooper admonishes the affluent black male
clergy to help those who have not been as successful as they in their material gains, sustaining her critique of the isolationist ambitions of some
black leaders (both male and female) who "exhaust their genius splitting
hairs on aristocratic distinctions and thanking God they are not as others"
(33). Here Cooper demonstrates, in an early period, a hallmark feature of
African American religious thought that will find expression in later figures: in order for all to flourish, the needs of each must be acknowledged
and met. She constantly warns against a rampant individualism that denies
the collective good, and she deplores a politics of favoritism that glosses
over the realities of intersectional oppression:

> But our present record of eminent men, when placed beside the actual
> status in America to-day, proves that no man can represent the race.
> Whatever the attainments of the individual may be . . . he can never be
> regarded as identical or representative of the whole. Not by pointing to
> sun-bathed mountain tops do we prove that Phoebus warms the valleys.
> We must point to homes, average homes, homes of the rank and file of
> horny handed toiling men and women of the South (where the masses
> are) lighted and cheered by the good, the beautiful, and the true,—
> then and not till then will the whole plateau be lifted into the sunlight.
> (30–31)

Cooper's theme of the interplay of one and all placed paramount emphasis on relationality as a metaphor constitutive of nature's reality; moreover,
this theme structures her feminist, pious, and cultural critiques aimed at

promoting equality in life for all humans. It is also exemplified in Cooper's view of women and men perfecting themselves with the ingestion of rich forms of knowledge and good, kind actions toward one another. More-over, her humanistic discourse was specifically aimed at enlivening the will of African Americans in ongoing efforts to claim and fulfill their humanity. With such rhetorical gestures, Cooper fleshes out Whitehead's notion that all livings things are characterized by a threefold urge: to live, to live well, to live better.[35] As I argue in the next two chapters, Cooper's efforts to en-noble African Americans' lives amid myriad dehumanizing processes are further advanced in distinct ways by W. E. B. Du Bois and James Baldwin. Tracing this general theme in their collective work underscores the intel-lectual trajectory that both anticipates and informs the concept of sacred humanity I develop.

CHAPTER 4

W. E. B. Du Bois: Humans as Centers of Value and Creativity

I have stepped within the Veil, raising it that you may view faintly
its deeper recesses,—the meaning of its religion, the passion
of its human sorrow, and the struggle of its greater souls.

—W. E. B. Du Bois, "The Forethought," *The Souls of Black Folk*

Anna Julia Cooper's keen sense of the interconnectedness of human life
was a major theme in the essays collected in *A Voice from the South*. Cooper
rejected an isolationist approach to the issues of racism, sexism, and class
differentiation in the United States as she made important connections
between natural processes and human flourishing. Furthermore, her use of
naturalistic imagery to advance the interplay of "one and all" resulted in a
rich conceptual framework that foreshadowed a crucial aspect of the religious ideal I sketched in the first section: a capacious vision of deep human
relations grounded in a communal ontology. In this chapter, I also connect
W. E. B. Du Bois with aspects of the sacred humanity concept, exploring
the anti-supernatural tendencies and the subtleties of meaning in his religiosity. I have touched briefly on his general assessment of African American religion in "Of the Faith of the Fathers"; I now consider Du Bois's
emphasis on human ingenuity within the African American religious context, emphasizing his view of religion as a natural process generated by the
finite conditions of human life, or under the specter of raced living. These
intriguing aspects of Du Bois's anti-transcendental approaches to black religiosity dovetail with my own theoretical convictions, and I examine how

his forward-thinking views on black humanity align with my concept of human destinies as precious centers of value. Thus, as I did in the case of Cooper, I explore in selected writings of Du Bois a richer model of humanity than those conceived by the influential racial discourses of his era.

Du Bois and Raced Living (Humanity Compromised)

In his biography of Du Bois, David Levering Lewis portrays the scholar from his youth onward as possessing a heightened awareness that human identity is paradoxically grounded in various modalities of existence. In many of his writings, Du Bois wrote of his own identity as indelibly imprinted with "raced" and "classed" value systems endemic to the northeastern United States.[1] In a now-famous narrative from *The Souls of Black Folk*, Du Bois invites readers to relive with him his jarring awakening, in Great Barrington, Massachusetts in 1878, to existence as a raced being:

> I remember well when the shadow swept across me. I was a little thing, away up in the hills of New England, where the dark Housatonic winds between Hoosac and Taghkanic to the sea. In a wee wooden school-house, something put it into the boys' and girls' heads to buy gorgeous visiting-cards—ten cents a package—and exchange. The exchange was merry, till one girl, a tall newcomer, refused my card—refused it peremptorily, with a glance. Then it dawned upon me with a certain suddenness that I was different from the others; or like, mayhap, in heart and life, and longing, but shut out from their world by a vast veil.[2]

Du Bois offers a poignant sense of being shut out from his peers' world because of a perceived difference in his humanity, which he sharpens into one of the central problematics of his generation: the impact of constructed racialized subjectivities on one's experience of one's humanity. Theorizing from the particular to the general, or from his own lived experience to that of other blacks, Du Bois sums up his appraisal of the quintessential African American subjectivity at that time: "It is a peculiar sensation, this double-consciousness, this sense of always looking at one's self through the eyes of others, of measuring one's soul by the tape of a world that looks on in amused contempt and pity. One ever feels his two-ness,—an American, a Negro; two souls, two thoughts, two unreconciled strivings; two warring ideals in one dark body, whose dogged strength alone keeps it from being torn asunder."[3]

The socioeconomic structures, aesthetic standards, and political realities facing African Americans in the late nineteenth century compelled

Du Bois to make sense of this quandary, and to articulate the peculiarity of having one's humanity identified as a problem to be solved. With a critical consciousness that established him as one of the most influential theoreticians of race in the twentieth century, Du Bois argued that what many whites viewed as natural fixtures were in actuality the cumulative effects of ill-conceived racial constructions. He also targeted inequitable practices and unjust social conventions based on essentialist views of race, which led to increased poverty, illiteracy, and consignment to menial labor among African Americans. As Mary Keller has observed, Du Bois's writings recognized the momentous work that lay ahead for all who strove for racial justice, by precisely identifying the subjective struggles of individuals in relation to the socioeconomic systems within which those individuals were constrained.[4] Du Bois never ceased to lend his attention to the quandaries of racialized existence. Approaching the end of his life, he reflected that his life had its own deep significance as part of a problem, which he considered the "central problem of the greatest of the world's democracies and so the Problem of the future world."[5] Much of the scholarly focus on Du Bois's conceptualization of the problem of raced living is found in such fields as sociology, education, journalism, civil rights, and political theory; however, I think Du Bois's views on religiosity also contribute greatly and uniquely to this legacy.[6] This contention may come as a surprise to some readers because of the common notion among many scholars that Du Bois was anti-religious.

In his introduction to *Du Bois on Religion*, Phil Zuckerman states that Du Bois's relationship with religion is a complex one that cannot be easily categorized in familiar terms. I agree with Zuckerman for a number of reasons. First, the vast canon of Du Bois's writings (both published and unpublished) shows that his religious views evolved as he grew older; moreover, Du Bois's style of writing about religion often contained myriad rhetorical conventions and figures of speech that held complex, layered possibilities of meaning.[7] Theoretical claims are conjoined with aesthetic and pious expressions as Du Bois wrote about his own beliefs. Second, eloquent social commentary and piercing psychological insights abound as Du Bois discerned often contradictory elements in the lived experiences of both black and white Christians. Normative ethical assertions are also found in certain accounts in which Du Bois analyzes the structural, historical forms of Christianity practiced during his era. Third, Du Bois was simultaneously a champion and critic of institutionalized religion, specifically Christianity, viewing it as both sustaining and oppressive, nurturing as well as exploitative, and a close reading of his religious reflections shows how intimately intertwined they are with his thoughts on the problem of black identity, and, by extension, with his desire that black humanity flourish.[8]

Du Bois's positive assessments of religion include acknowledgments of its role in varied African American historical, sociopolitical, and aesthetic-ethical narratives, in which principles of liberation, social justice, and social ethics remain in the fore. In his groundbreaking study *The Philadelphia Negro: A Social Study* (1899), while assessing the myriad social problems (such as segregation, poverty, lack of education, and crime) affecting late-nineteenth-century freed African Americans, Du Bois does not fail to stress the sense of agency and self-determination among the founders of the African Methodist Episcopal (AME) Church of America. Its major contributions to black life at that time led Du Bois to describe the AME Church as "the most remarkable product of American Negro civilization."[9] One must also consider Du Bois's socioliterary and political views of Jesus, in which he makes an important analogy between the suffering Jesus and the suffering of blacks, anticipating later revolutionary Christological discourses in systematic works of black liberation theology. Furthermore, in his biography of John Brown, Du Bois accentuates the positive and pervasive impact religion had on the white abolitionist throughout his life. In the text, Du Bois sketches a positive view of Brown's revolutionary commitment and Christian martyrdom, praising Brown's keen sensibility in recognizing that blacks were fit to take care of themselves.[10]

Du Bois's perspectives on religion also included harsh critiques of its institutional failures, particularly those he associated with white Christian traditions. In personal correspondence in 1925, he offered scathing commentary on the Roman Catholic Church's systematic rejection of black students into its educational systems:

> The Catholic Church in America stands for color separation and discrimination to a degree equaled by no other church in America, and that is saying a very great deal. . . . The white parochial schools even in the North, exclude colored children, the Catholic University at Washington invites them elsewhere and scarcely a Catholic seminary in the country will train a Negro priest. This is not the case of blaming the Catholic Church for not doing all it might—it is blaming it for being absolutely and fundamentally wrong today and in the United States on the basic demands of human brotherhood across the color line.[11]

Anticipating the liberationist strains of black theology in the mid–twentieth century that were manifest in the life and work of such iconic figures as Martin Luther King, Jr. and James Cone, Du Bois also indicted white Christianity for its ineffectual social justice and its hypocrisy in addressing race relations. Its mainstream churches, he argued, professed the ideals of Christian love while consistently perpetuating systemic acts of violence both in America and elsewhere. He writes:

> It is painfully true that White Christianity has in the twentieth century been curiously discredited. Here in the twentieth century of the Prince of Peace the leading nations representing His religion have been murdering, maiming and hurting each other on a scale unprecedented in the history of Mankind. Again, into the White Church of Christ race prejudice has crept to such an extent it is openly recognized and in the United States at least it is considered the natural and normal thing that white and colored people should belong mostly to different organizations and almost entirely to different congregations. . . . These facts do not impugn Christianity but they do make terrible comment upon the failure of its white followers.[12]

Added to these critiques are Du Bois's later reprobations of the black church's hypocrisy toward its own members. He spoke often of the moral failures of its leaders in making black folk "ashamed of themselves" and "invoking false means of salvation."[13]

As he acknowledged in one of his last autobiographical writings, Du Bois's critiques of institutional religion, inclusive of both white and black Christianity, increased as he matured as an intellectual:

> At 17 I was in a missionary college where religious orthodoxy was stressed; but I was more developed to meet it with argument, which I did. . . . By the time of graduation I was still a "believer" in orthodox religion, but had strong questions which were encouraged at Harvard. In Germany I became a freethinker and when I came to teach at an orthodox Methodist negro school I was soon to regard it with suspicion, especially when I refused to lead the students in public prayer. When I became head of a department in Atlanta, the engagement was held up because I balked at leading in prayer. . . . From my 30th year on I have increasingly regarded the church as an institution which defended such evils as slavery, color caste, exploitation of labor and war.[14]

The thirty-year marker Du Bois mentions is notable, as it inaugurates a critical juncture of his life (1898 onward) when he is increasingly developing his role as a social justice activist and leader of racial progress in the United States. This shift in his identity was inflected by his studies in Germany, where Du Bois saw the appeal of socialist principles and also witnessed the popularity of race theories based on evolutionary themes. He returned to the United States with a deeper appreciation of the wider, global set of issues involved in confronting the race problem.

Lewis describes the country that Du Bois returned to as one dominated by a national white consensus view of African Americans as inferior human beings whose predicament was three parts of their own making and two parts the consequence of misguided white philanthropy. Skewed views of blacks' humanity were bountiful in the scholarly productions of the time, including anthropological perspectives that positioned blacks "somewhere on the frontier between the great apes and homo sapiens," biological studies that considered blacks' "average brain weight less than Caucasians'," and psychological works describing a "primal sexuality and irrationality" in blacks that were supposedly exacerbated by stress.[15] Within this cultural milieu, Du Bois "resolved to write of the genius, humanity, and enviable destiny of his race with such passion, eloquence, and penetration that claims of African American inferiority would be sent reeling, never to recover full legitimacy and vitality, despite their enormous resiliency."[16] In 1903 *The Souls of Black Folk* was published, which placed black genius and vitality at the center of African American life and expressed black self-determination. Du Bois joined forces with William Monroe Trotter in 1905 to form the Niagara Movement, which transformed into the NAACP in 1909, to develop a plan for aggressive action that demanded suffrage, equal economic and educational opportunities, an end to segregation, and full civil rights. Du Bois also became editor of *The Horizon: A Journal of the Color Line*, which emphasized socialist perspectives as it sought to cover the global world behind and beyond "the veil."

These important developments provide the backdrop for understanding some of Du Bois's critiques of traditional African American religion. He accentuated the vacuity of traditional African American religious symbolism and practices, deploring adherents' misplaced emphasis on faith as belief in myths. On numerous occasions, he described Christianity as an influential system that fostered blind acceptance of doctrines rather than critical thinking. In short, Du Bois perpetually questioned taken-for-granted norms, and he demythologized presumed *a priori* truths and beliefs upheld by the black church. A commencement speech at Fisk University that Du Bois delivered to the class of 1938 encapsulates these critical sensibilities about the black church: "It has built up a body of dogma and fairy tale, fantastic fables of sin and salvation, impossible creeds and impossible demands for unquestioning belief and obedience."[17] As these examples suggest, Du Bois recognized the human constructions that lay behind organized religion, as well as the power religion had to shape human lives—for good or for ill.

Placing Du Bois within Religious Naturalism

The complexity and range of perspectives on religion held by Du Bois could support any number of interpretations regarding his own religiosity. In this study, I place Du Bois's views within the context of an African American religious naturalism, further advancing a general idea expressed by Jonathon Kahn in his important and timely text, *Divine Discontent: The Religious Imagination of W. E. B. Du Bois*.[18] In the growing body of literature assessing Du Bois's relation to religion, Kahn's work provides a new reading of Du Bois that warrants attention. Kahn first contends that Du Bois's discontent with religion and divinity is nicely encapsulated in an address Du Bois delivered at Wilberford University in 1940, forty years after he had taught there in his first academic position. Commenting on the place of Christianity at Wilberforce, Du Bois asserts, "I have noted in your president's report the insistence that Wilberforce University is a Christian institution. This is an old note. . . . It was a matter of emphasis when I was here nearly a half century ago and it did not impress me because it was all too evident that what most people at Wilberforce called Christianity was childish belief in fairy tales, a word-of-mouth adherence to dogma, and a certain sectarian exclusiveness."[19] As Kahn notes, the Wilberforce address contains the familiar elements of Du Bois's anticlericalism, his suspicion of religious dogma, and his outrage at black Christianity's hypocrisy and failure to help the poor and disenfranchised. Yet Kahn insists, and I agree with his assessment, that it is a mistake to focus exclusively on Du Bois's anticlericalism, or even on his doubts about normative Christian supernatural commitments, as conclusive evidence of Du Bois's lack of religiosity. Rather, Kahn situates Du Bois's religious perspectives within a pragmatic religious naturalism that extends from William James through George Santayana to John Dewey. Kahn asserts:

> The central complications of Du Bois' religious register—tension between religious disbelief and devotion, refusal to attribute earthly events to divine metaphysics, construction of identity, peoplehood, and nation from the lived exigencies of race and not racial essences, as well as pursuit of an earthly form of human salvation rooted in human relations rather than antecedent realities—mirror basic pragmatic

commitments. Moreover, they set Du Bois outside of normative black Christianity.[20]

Rather than set up a divide between the religious Du Bois and the anti-religious Du Bois, Kahn investigates the subtleties of religious meaning in Du Bois's rhetorical and theoretical gestures. Notably, Kahn argues that when Du Bois speaks religiously—whether using God talk, praying, or even referring to Christ—it is not to confirm the existence of a supernatural divine order. Rather, nodding in the direction of Wittgenstein, Kahn states that Du Bois's use of the modalities of religion are religious insofar as they bear resemblance to other language uses, ideas, and narratives that are distinctly representative of religion. Kahn further associates Du Bois's entanglements of social criticism, racial theories, and values discourse with what he calls Du Bois's religious imagination, or, more specifically, Du Bois's divine discontent.[21] Whereas some scholars might use the phrase "divine discontent" to promote a view of Du Bois's atheism and his total rejection of religion, Kahn advances it to capture Du Bois's critical sensibilities toward current configurations of political and social life.

In Kahn's reading, "divinity—religious language, ideas, narratives, and virtues—becomes in Du Bois's hands a tool to express discontent" at what exists in order to transform it into a this-worldly ideal.[22] In Du Bois's embracing of black religious ideals there is a basic orientation and fundamental conviction that transformation of the human and of our diverse world-formations are possible; however, these aspirations are primarily achieved in and through human efforts—in the here and now. There are no supernatural or metaphysical realities that supersede or ground such actions. Rather, within the complexities of black culture and life, Du Bois's religiosity unfolds as a strain of pragmatic religious naturalism insofar as Du Bois shows that "religion is valuable, even essential, for the way it provides humans with ways to address and reconcile themselves with the natural limits of human experience."[23]

I follow Kahn's general direction in arguing that Du Bois's anti-metaphysical leanings yield a unique mode of religiosity that falls within the purview of religious naturalism. However, in doing so, I advance another argument for understanding and advancing this claim. As indicated in chapter 2, my approach to religious naturalism is informed by current scientific studies that focus on the emergence and value of human life within a larger matrix of natural processes. Utilizing this vein of religious naturalism, I posited an expanded understanding of the human, using various explanatory and interpretive frameworks devoid of supernatural or transcendent notions. I conceptualized human life forms as natural, value-laden processes in deep relationship with other natural processes, constituting the sacrality of human life. Accordingly, my sense of what constitutes the *religious* in religious naturalism is that it is inextricably connected to the question of what it means to be human in a particular way. Thus, in returning to Du Bois, I contend that the category of religiousness that Du Bois uses (including, in this context, his evocations of the divine) is not only or merely a pragmatic tool that accentuates human transformation; it can also be viewed as an interpretive framework that focuses on how individuals and communities "humanize" ourselves as value-laden organisms. Within the immediate contexts of raced living—in which blacks were constantly subjected to dehumanizing practices—the quintessential religious task of Du Bois's day, the new ideal he evokes, is expanding on what it means *to be human* in such a way that certain forms of transformation can occur. It is in this context that I argue for Du Bois's contributions to an emerging African American religious naturalism.

Du Bois's Antimetaphysical Sensibilities and Nontheological Rhetoric

Du Bois was not a philosopher of religion or a constructive theologian, and consequently he did not write a systematic theory outlining his basic convictions. In light of this observation, I think it is impossible to identify in his writings a thoroughgoing antimetaphysical epistemology. Yet it is very clear that Du Bois offered fairly consistent comments revealing his distrust of traditional Christian doctrines based on metaphysical speculation. Many of these assertions are found either in public speeches or in the personal correspondence of his later years, in which Du Bois repeatedly denied his adherence to commonly shared Christian doctrines. In a letter written at the age of sixty-nine, Du Bois writes: "I am not a member of a Christian church; although I have been at times in the past; I do not subscribe to ordinary Christian doctrine."[24] At other times, he was more specific in his rejection of a doctrine, while endorsing some type of empiricism. For example, in one very brief piece, Du Bois responded to the eschatological affirmations of basic Christian doctrines with a robust agnosticism: "My thought on immortality is easily explained. I do not know. I do not see how anyone could know. Our whole basis of knowledge is so relative and contingent that when we get to argue concerning ultimate reality and the real essence of life and the past and the future, we seem to be talking without real data and getting nowhere."[25] With this passage, Du Bois offers both commonsense empiricism and epistemological humility at the lack of evidence for traditional eschatological claims; at the same time, he rejects the dogmatism of militant atheism, which would "deny the possibility of future life," with the admission that "I have no knowledge of the possibilities of this universe and I know of no one who has."[26] Here, we have a nice example of Du Bois's skepticism toward sanctioned Christian tenets; and yet, at the same time, this passage is also an interesting expression of his naturalism. Du Bois makes references to the expansive, unfolding, complex workings of the universe rather than succumbing to a dogmatism that requires the suspension of one's cognitive faculties. This sense of awe and wonder at natural phenomenon is a sentiment often shared among contemporary religious naturalists.

Du Bois's refutation of historical Christianity was sometimes extended to other traditions, as evinced in this passage in one letter: "There is no religion of which I know whose dogma and creed is one in which I wholly believe. I do not believe in the existence and rulership of the one God of the Jews; I do not believe in the miraculous birth and the miracles of the Christ of the Christians. I do not believe in many of the tenets of Mohammedanism and Buddhism."[27] In this passage, one senses in Du Bois a healthy skepticism toward any model of faith as uncritical assent to a set of basic, fundamental convictions that are passed on through prescribed, sanctioned interpretations, or tradition. Du Bois's critique is similar to that of many contemporary thinkers who see the sterility of institutional religion when it has ceased to advance human dignity and failed to promote critical thinking. In this sense, his suspicion participates in the model of religious naturalism I espouse, which inspires one to question outdated models of religion based on propositional truth claims grounded in divine revelation and passed on via the proper institutional mechanisms. With his socialist sensibilities, Du Bois unmasked an influential model of religion as an oppressive tool that thwarts critical inquiry with its demands of strict adherence to doctrinal purity and its confessional devotion to "folk tales of children without fathers, of death which was life, of sacrifice which was shrewd investment and ridiculous pictures of an endless future."[28] In correspondence with various individuals, he consistently expressed skepticism toward traditional teachings that demanded suspension of one's critical skills. In a letter of 1925 to a friend, Du Bois even articulated a naturalistic reading of biblical texts: "I do not believe that the biblical record is authentic history, I think it is very interesting myth and legend."[29]

As stated earlier, Du Bois did not offer in his writings a systematic epistemology of key Christian doctrines, as would a philosopher or scholar of religion. At the same time, he became increasingly wary of the influence of

Christian indoctrination on many Americans, noting its power of persuasion over those who failed to exercise their cognitive faculties. Du Bois also recognized the failures of Christianity as a cultural force insofar as it did not help its adherents develop moral integrity in terms of social justice. This orientation seems consistent with his outlook as he matured in age. In his last autobiography, Du Bois lauded the Soviet Union for not allowing any church of any kind to interfere with education and religion in the public schools; notably, within the United States he observed that "many folk follow religious ceremonies and services; and allow their children to learn fairy tales and so-called religious truth, which in time the children come to recognize as conventional lies. . . . One can hardly exaggerate the moral disaster of this custom."[30]

Du Bois's skepticism also extended to traditional theistic claims. An interesting passage often cited by scholars is found in a 1948 response to a query from E. Pino Moreno, a Cuban priest, who was curious about Du Bois's theological views:

> Answering your letter of October 3, may I say: If by being "a believer in God," you mean a belief in a person of vast power who consciously rules the universe for the good of mankind, I answer No; I cannot disprove this assumption, but I certainly see no proof to sustain such a belief, neither in History nor in my personal experience. If on the other hand you mean by "God" a vague Force which, in some incomprehensible way, dominates all life and change, then I answer, Yes; I recognize such Force, and if you wish to call it God, I do not object.[31]

This ambiguous passage has generated various responses from scholars, and many have used it to either support their sense of Du Bois's theistic orientation, or to deny altogether that he had one. For example, while conceding that Du Bois is a rational social scientist, Dwight Hopkins yet imagines that Du Bois's faith is capacious enough to embrace things that are not completely understandable. According to Hopkins, Du Bois's "Force" or God is an incomprehensible holiness grounded in human affairs, empowering humanity to take initiative in social transformation.[32] While interpreting the "Force" that Du Bois references in a nonorthodox manner, Hopkins yet reinscribes it with theistic overtones: "Du Bois had faith in a Force or God that labored alongside and empowered humanity to work for a new democracy and politics. This was his ultimate concern in life—and the concept of God as Force let him maintain his faith. For him, God revealed divinity among people who gave their lives for the subjugated of this world."[33] Unfortunately, Hopkins fails to specify the content and nature of the Du Boisian God that is this Force, which leads me to ponder how one could give such an explicit theological rendering to the passage. In short, I cannot share Hopkins's theological zeal and attribute specific theistic content to an ambiguous term that Du Bois himself did not define or elaborate on in his writings.

Rather than arguing whether or not Du Bois was an atheist or a theist, which I think is futile given his lack of systematic theological reflection, I prefer to focus on a discernible pattern in his writings. As noted, there are many instances of antimetaphysical leanings in his writings and work, and even when he employs theistic language, as in the above passage, it is often cast in ambiguous or vague terms. Alongside these critiques is Du Bois's continued emphasis on human efforts to transform the adverse effects of raced living. What this suggests to me is that Du Bois's religious rhetoric does not fully or consistently support the determination or assertion of a transcendental, suprahistorical agent who is solely responsible for African Americans. Rather, in keeping with Du Bois's socialist sensibilities and his ongoing emphasis on human ingenuity within the context of raced living in the United States, I think it is important to focus on his conception of a self-determined black humanity governed by a sense of purposive living. In the next section, I consider Du Bois's religiosity in this context, describing it as an exercise in values discourse in relation to the human ingenuity that he champions. What will be crucial in my discussion is Du Bois's grasp of religiosity itself.

Reconstructing the Human as a Religious Task

Given that Du Bois did not systematize his antimetaphysical leanings and convictions, one viable approach to gauging his religiosity is grasping the theoretical subtleties of his sustained (re)focus on the human beings who make such transcendental claims. Within the context of the problem he identified at the turn of the twentieth century, Du Bois focused again and again on the merits of human ingenuity, instead of relying on speculative, transcendental ideals. As I argued in chapter 2, religious naturalism's awareness of human finitude without an appeal to some suprahistorical deity brings into sharper focus a view of the human as a center of value that seeks its own flourishing. I see Du Bois's religiosity as constituted within this conceptual space, namely, in his supplanting of traditional theistic (or metaphysical) renderings with a keen, capacious appreciation of humanity—and, specifically, black humanity. Anthony Pinn articulates this same point in a slightly different way: "Du Bois understood religion as entailing deep feelings for life, a connection to the fundamental impulses of existence that shape how we understand and live life. . . . He had to address the various ways in which the human response to these deep feelings and fundamental impulses is expressed in the mundane activities of life and in the normal development of African-American culture."[34] Although Du Bois did not offer a systematic, constructive theoretical framework, as I have done in chapters 1 and 2 above, his religiosity was a rich affirmation of life, or an uncompromising claim to life, imbued with humanistic values and cultural currency. On more than one occasion, he identified self-determinacy and moral agency as key factors circumscribing human life as meaningful and imbued with telos. In a 1956 letter to Herbert Aptheker, Du Bois writes:

> I assumed that human beings could alter and re-direct the course
> of events as to better human conditions. I knew that this power was
> limited by environment, inheritance and natural law, and that from the
> point of view of science these occurrences must be a matter of Chance
> and not of Law. I did not rule out the possibility of some God also
> influencing and directing human action and natural law. However I saw
> no evidence of such divine guidance. I did see evidence of the decisive
> action of human beings.[35]

As this example makes clear, Du Bois often makes a conceptual move beyond speculative supernatural theistic reflection to focus on the human organism—in my view, the human animal as a center of value that is self-determinate in its relations with others.

As some critics have noted, *The Souls of Black Folk* remains a rich text for those wishing to explore Du Bois's religiosity; for example, Kahn suggests that in this work one sees that Du Bois gives up "the search for the transcendental in religion and instead understands religion as a naturalistic practice, as a historical product of human interpretation of conditions of finitude."[36] In the book Du Bois uses traditional religious imagery and biblical metaphors that would be very apparent to many African American and white Christians. However, in Du Bois's hands, the religious rhetoric and imagery are not mere adaptations of Christian teachings, but rather a call to blacks to enact a fuller existential task: naming and embracing their humanity. This language specifically champions the integrity of blacks exercising their humanity and creating various forms of transformative praxis. To illustrate this point, I return to Du Bois's notion of life within the veil, where he speaks of the double-consciousness that accompanies the conflictual sense of self—a divided self—experienced by African Americans.

In "Of Our Spiritual Strivings," a pivotal essay in *The Souls of Black Folk*, Du Bois argues that the history of Africans on this continent is the history of this strife—also known as the perceived "problem" of the African for white culture. While naming the discriminatory practices and moral deficiencies of a nation that has thwarted blacks' movement toward achieving their full humanity, Du Bois reminds African Americans of the task set before them; he also reprimands white Americans for denying blacks the opportunities to do so. In a key passage, he declares: "This, then, is the end of his striving: to be a co-worker in the kingdom of culture, to escape both death and isolation, to husband and use his best powers and latent genius."[37] As Anna Julia Cooper had so eloquently done, Du Bois evokes the innate genius of black humans aspiring to actualize themselves. With this passage, Du Bois voices a prophetic call for African Americans to bear witness to themselves as authentic beings; it is a message ingeniously embedded in the admixture of biblical, cultural, and rhetorical gestures outlining the progress of Africans on the new continent. In the essay he also alludes to a particular image of Jesus in the Synoptic Gospels, teaching his disciples about the kingdom of God; he encourages them to be fruitful laborers and to escape the current corrupt world order by developing talents within themselves.

In *The Souls of Black Folk* Du Bois consistently characterizes blacks as beings with an innate desire for subjectivity. This desire is one of the hallmarks of existential humanism, as it is that capacity in humans which allow us to make our claim on life. Du Bois also makes clear to the reader that blacks have been incessant dreamers of ontological integrity—what I described earlier as blacks recognizing themselves as vital, intrinsic centers of value.[38] The implication is that even when enslaved, African Americans' designation as objects in dominant white culture was held in tension with their ardent desire for transcendence. To be subjects of history in the classic Sartrean sense was the goal, and this meant their devotion to a noble human ideal—freedom—elevated to divine status. In "Of Our Spiritual Strivings" Du Bois observes, "Away back in the days of bondage they thought to see in one divine event the end of all doubt and disappointment; few men ever worshipped Freedom with half such unquestioning faith as did the American Negro for two centuries" (366).

Du Bois also outlines the various means by which African Americans, doubly constituted by two impulses (or experiencing a conflicted sense of self), have sought to create and sustain for themselves their own harmoniously grounded humanity—in short, to be authors of their own destinies. In general philosophic terms, coming to terms with our humanity has important moral and ethical implications for rational beings. It involves positing constitutive subjectivities capable of constructing assorted judgments that bring together our knowledge of "what is" and our expectations of "what ought to be." In my theoretical framework of religious naturalism, I describe this as an instance of human valuing, in which an integrative understanding of human desires and perceptions helps constitute us as relational, becoming entities. In the process, human animals are concerned with posing and answering the following questions: What is true? What ought to be? How ought we to act? What may be good for us? For what may we hope? Why live at all? These questions, I argue, are essential to Du Bois's positioning of African American life within the veil. They are integral to his conception of a black humanity that recognizes its existence as a problem, that lives the quandary of a divided, false sense of self denied access to true subjectivity, which increases the longing "to merge [its] double self into a better and truer self" ("Of Our Spiritual Strivings," 365).

Du Bois employed, as did Cooper and other black visionaries, tropes from antiquity to convey the qualities of a decaying culture in which "slavery was indeed the sum of all villainies, the cause of all sorrow, the root of all prejudice" (366). He also sketches in the essay a fascinating coming-of-age narrative for black consciousness in search of itself. Accordingly, he describes the basic capacity to vote in the United States as a vital mechanism in the hands of African Americans in pursuit of their full humanity: "The ballot, which before he had looked upon as a visible sign of freedom, he now regarded as the chief means of gaining and perfecting the liberty with which war had partially endowed him" (367). Beyond acknowledging the power of enfranchisement signified by voting rights, Du Bois was adamant that gaining the ballot was a stage in self-determination (a stage in entering into the kingdom of culture), which he ingeniously associates with entering Canaan, the land of promise for the ancient Israelites. Thus, in outlining an epic narrative that details the passage from bondage to emancipation, or from existing in a mode of objectivity to that of subjectivity, Du Bois associates with blacks the central task of nation-building that biblical archaeologists often describe as embedded in the sacred literature of the Israelites. This narrative incorporates a founding myth, pivotal or symbolic events, and iconic figures who represent the culture's ideals, dreams, inspirations, and sense of destiny. For Du Bois, however, within the confines of racialized existence, the historical progress in this salvific unfolding will not be fully complete until African Americans begin to envision themselves as authentic beings belonging to themselves (and not to some deity outside of themselves). This realization occurs when African

Americans begin to target the true source of their misery: racial injustice wrought by an immoral white culture preoccupied with its arbitrary ontological constructions. For Du Bois, such an awareness, or coming of age of black consciousness, entails blacks necessarily embracing their full, vital humanity, their claiming ontological integrity for themselves. In describing this critical consciousness within black humans destined to claim their lives, Du Bois asserts:

> [I]t changed the child of Emancipation to the youth with dawning self-consciousness, self-realization, self-respect. In those sombre forests of his striving his own soul rose before him, and he saw himself,—darkly as through a veil; and yet he saw in himself some faint revelation of his power, of his mission. He began to have a dim feeling that, to attain his place in the world, he must be himself, and not another. For the first time he sought to analyze the burden he bore upon his back, that dead-weight of social degradation partially masked behind a half-named Negro problem. (368)

Du Bois's Religious Mandate: Embodying One Value

More definitively than most other humanistic discourses, the discipline of religion has demonstrated that the process of valuing is an inevitable and necessary dimension of being human. Religious valuing implies that we humans are capable of reflecting on aspects of our subjectivity, which, for African Americans living inside the veil, has been constituted as a "distorted" unity, distinct from the unity often assumed by white Americans. Du Bois's religiosity advances this truth. He consistently shows African Americans desiring a sense of their essential, whole humanity, and, beyond this, seeking standards of virtue for the various tasks we apply to ourselves as we relate to others. In this sense, his various claims in addressing the "black problem" may be viewed as an early form of religious valuing that confronts the ills of modernity as a race-plagued episteme. "I very early got the idea," Du Bois told an interviewer from Columbia University, "that what I was going to do was to prove to the world that Negroes were just like other people."[39] Du Bois's theories and convictions regarding African Americans' self-determination, self-actualization, and aspirations toward becoming their own humanity began with his own enactment of it. Moreover, the various controversies with which Du Bois was involved showed the level of personal excellence that he imagined possible—for himself, for African Americans, for North America. He cultivated a love of

black humanity and what it could symbolize at a time when it was anathema
to do so.

During high school, Du Bois became an avid proponent of racial pride,
showing his concern for the elevation of the race—a common concern
among nineteenth-century African American leaders and thinkers. As a
local correspondent for the *New York Globe*, at the age of fifteen Du Bois
wrote lectures and editorials that urged black communities to politicize
themselves. Biographies of Du Bois and his autobiographies often give
accounts of his awareness of his intellectual gifts, and the pride he felt
in surpassing his fellow white students in academic and other pursuits. In
1888, evoking a mystical sense of calling and employing biblical imagery,
Du Bois asserted: "Through the leadership of men like myself and my fellows, we were going to have these enslaved Israelites out of the still enduring bondage in short order," and later, in 1890, while studying in Berlin, he
wrote in a diary: "These are my plans: to make a name in science, to make
a name in literature, and thus to raise my race. Or perhaps to raise a visible
empire in Africa. . . . And if I perish—I perish."[40]

These reflections lead me to suggest that when we think about Du Bois's
religious valuing, we are acknowledging at least minimally a fundamental
human propensity toward life that features distinctive cognitive and emotive elements. Uniting cognition and affectivity as inseparable elements of
religious valuing departs from empiricist approaches that focus exclusively
on religious knowledge. Accordingly, my sense of Du Bois's religious valuing is that it is not directed toward tendencies to seek the "essence" of
"true religiosity" in a faith that is understood only as a divine gift, or toward a belief system that provides a normative vocabulary for its adherents.
Nor can one conclude easily that his *primary* aim was to challenge those
explanations of religious valuing as merely a by-product of social and psychological processes, a by-product that has, at best, instrumental value, or,
at worse, is a superstitious survival from earlier times. In this regard, *The
Souls of Black Folk* is a multifarious text, one that can be read on a number
of levels. As Pinn suggests, "Albeit central, the question of 'how does it feel
to be a problem?' captures only a portion of the book's premise, because
Du Bois is also concerned with the creative unraveling of black humanity
as it occurs in the more opaque areas of African American life. *Souls* offers
a soft assertion that black bodies have 'weight' or 'soul' not fully accounted
for through talk of the existential dimensions of race and race relations."[41]

In Du Bois, one finds a different kind of religious awakening: a naturalistic take on the legacy of a vibrant religiosity that has incessantly in-

sisted on naming and celebrating black humanity as essential and valuable. Du Bois certainly kept his eyes on the proper prize: ennobled black humans who refused to give up on life and strove to make it theirs. In returning once again to the insider-outsider trope, we should not forget a crucial point: Du Bois's very early conception of life within the veil was always accompanied by his imagining the possibilities of life beyond it. The ongoing inspiration he provided to his contemporaries was inextricably tied to his image of African Americans as centers of value whose self-generating genius and potency had become obfuscated by the veil. Not only this, but Du Bois sketched out a comprehensive, multifaceted approach to the social problems facing his generation:

> Work, culture, liberty,—all these we need, not singly but together, not successively but together, each growing and aiding each, and all striving toward that vaster ideal that swims before the Negro people, the ideal of human brotherhood, gained through the unifying ideal of Race; the ideal of fostering and developing the traits and talents of the Negro, not in opposition to or contempt for other races, but rather in large conformity to the ideals of the American Republic, in order that some day on American soil two world-races may give each to each those characteristics both so sadly lack. ("Of Our Spiritual Strivings," 370)

Du Bois's vision of black humanity beyond the veil reverberates with historic significance, both for its articulation of late-nineteenth-century optimism and its provocative religious notion that black humanity is essential humanity.

CHAPTER 5

James Baldwin: Religion, Race, and the Love of Humanity

Love takes off masks that we fear we cannot live
without and know we cannot live within.

Love does not begin and end the way we seem to think it
does. Love is a battle, love is a war; love is a growing up.

—JAMES BALDWIN, "In Search of a Majority"

As long as certain configurations of the world exist—what some of us identify as asymmetrical social and power relations among human beings—there is a need for alternative cultural values and ethical mandates. Anna Julia Cooper and W. E. B. Du Bois absorbed this insight and encouraged their contemporaries to recognize the transitory, fallible nature of racial constructions embedded in essentialist notions of human superiority and inferiority. Their critiques of American life focused on perceived, sacrosanct "truths" about blacks' humanity, which they questioned, disassembled, and, in some cases, even reconstructed in their published work. Such theoretical acuity is also reflected in the writings of James Baldwin, the third iconic figure I associate with the concept of sacred humanity. Baldwin, too, dreamt of brave new conceptions of humanity beyond the vexed, raced configurations he both experienced and witnessed in the United States; in his writings, he ingeniously unmasked racial, heterosexual, and other problematic privileges lurking in dominant constructions of the human in North American culture and religion.[1]

In this chapter, I focus on Baldwin's efforts during the mid–twentieth century to enhance race relations in the United States with an expanded view of humanity and our capacity to love one another.[2] As a scriptor of human possibilities, he wrote about the alienating effects of race hatred in North America, using frank, often provocative language to convey his thoughts. With an eye toward expanding his contemporaries' views of their constitutive humanity, Baldwin also emphasized embodied forms of love that he believed would result in the vital flourishing of all North Americans. Far from being a lofty abstraction, Baldwin's conception of love entailed a radical adjustment of human relations, requiring individuals and communities to embrace others they often feared, dismissed, or even hated. Within the context of the U.S. civil rights era, Baldwin's concept of love specifically demanded from whites and blacks unprecedented acts of courage and audacious choices.

Drawing primarily from his works of nonfiction, I explore the theoretical subtleties of Baldwin's concept of love within the context of raced living in the United States. I connect this concept to the axiological import and symbolic meanings he associates with the constructions of whiteness and blackness inhering in religious and cultural systems. I also address Baldwin's sense of the existential tasks involved in both blacks' and whites' embracing of blackness as a goal toward achieving both national and individual well being.[3] Seen from this vantage point, Baldwin's perspectives augment Cooper's earlier ontological concerns found in her "one and all" discourse, and his rhetoric reflects some of Du Bois's sensibilities that African Americans' authentic humanity had become obfuscated in complicated renderings of raced living in the United States. Accordingly, this chapter furthers my premise that collectively as well as individually, these three thinkers imagined what human beings could be, beyond what their respective generations experienced or envisioned. Their ideas, posited from the late nineteenth century through the mid-twentieth, constitute a trajectory of thinking that helped to usher in the expanded view of humanity I posit with my conception of sacred humanity: humans as intrinsically relational, natural organisms motivated by a desire for goodness and connection with all that is. More specifically, within black culture, as did Cooper and Du Bois in their distinct ways, Baldwin, too, augments my sense of black humans as lovers of life and vital centers of value at a critical time in American history.

Race, Religion, and Baldwin

Baldwin is noted for his provocative works of literature that in their beauty and depth remain essential parts of the American canon. Within the con-

text of the fraught cultural dynamics of the 1950s through the 1980s, however, Baldwin's achievements as a writer exceed his literary greatness. In
drawing on his experiences, whether as a teenage preacher, a gay man,
a black expatriate, a public intellectual, or an activist in the struggle for
civil rights, Baldwin keenly perceived the alienating effects of raced living.
From *Go Tell It on the Mountain* (1953), Baldwin's acclaimed first novel, to
The Evidence of Things Not Seen (1985), his last published work, the iconic
writer fused historical meditations and personal insights with keen cultural
analyses of myriad forms of social injustice and racial prejudice.

Baldwin wrote passionately about the quandaries of living life as an out-
lier. In *Notes of a Native Son* (1955) and other writings, he brought an in-
tense self-awareness to inhabiting within one body many different (and often polarized) cultural markers. In the America of his day, these identities
were persistently viewed as oppositional: his blackness and erotic-affective
desires; his precocious religious insights and radical activism; his designation as a black American artist in Europe juxtaposed with his European
celebrity in white America. In his quest to create an authentic mode of
existence, however, Baldwin resisted, with varying degrees of success, the
easy option of allowing others to reduce his capacious humanity to any single identity. Furthermore, he creatively expanded this sensibility to include
the collective experiences of African Americans as he sought new ways of
being in which he and others could live fully with perceived differences.

In their introduction to a critical collection of essays on Baldwin, Cora
Kaplan and Bill Schwartz describe a dominant trend in Baldwin studies that
often has failed to understand this point. As they observe, "For too long
one Baldwin has been pitted against another Baldwin, producing a series
of polarities that has skewed our understanding: his art against his politics,
his fiction against his nonfiction; his early writings against his late writings;
American Baldwin against European Baldwin; black Baldwin against queer
Baldwin."[4] I share their own more robust reading of Baldwin. Select essays
written by Baldwin show him resisting facile, externally imposed views of
his humanity, as well as that of other blacks. Baldwin opened an imaginative space in which Americans trapped in isolationist encampments could
be free and re-envision themselves as relational beings capable of living
with difference. In the 1984 introduction to *Notes of a Native Son*, Baldwin
described the menacing effects of racialized living in America. Symbolically, socially, and materially, human lives were affected by a problematic
cultural system that elevated certain bodies over others, ultimately leav-
ing all alienated from one another. For Baldwin, racialized existence in
its most extreme form was expressed in a black-white oppositional logic

that was omnipresent: "The conundrum of color is the inheritance of every American, be he/she legally or actually Black or White. It is a fearful inheritance, for which untold multitudes, long ago, sold their birthright. Multitudes are doing so, until today."[5] Baldwin's writings reverberate with the truth of affirming life and embracing one's humanity in a world (or a culture of values) that one has not created.

Baldwin was particularly sensitive to the problematic configurations of blackness and whiteness that were often held in place by religious ideals and conventions. His writings include essays that reveal Baldwin's adeptness in showing that different, competing versions of reality are tied to specific views of humanity, and this theoretical insight underscores a central feature of Baldwin's cultural critique of American racism and why he ties it to religion. He often depicts intimate, often troubling connections between dominant constructions of racial identity and the fixed structures of transcendent religious ideals operating in the American psyche; as I discuss later, for Baldwin, this particular amalgamation was a stumbling block for those wishing to embrace their authentic humanity. Accordingly, he believed a dynamic, radical conception of love between individuals and among diverse communities had to be enacted within the vicissitudes of raced living. Equally important was Baldwin's conviction that this form of love was often absent from traditional forms of religiosity. These convictions, I contend, help to explain why Baldwin consistently focused on religious imagery and ideas in his writings, in spite of his movement away from traditional black religiosity.

As was true for Du Bois, Baldwin's relationship to organized religion was layered and complex. Within literary studies, various scholars have addressed the problem of identifying Baldwin as a religious writer and grasping his relationship with structured religion or Christianity. One notable trend in Baldwin studies has been the shift from an essential lack of acknowledgement of religion in Baldwin in the sixties to the later focus on his extensive use of religious imagery, with critics either celebrating its presence or pronouncing Baldwin a secular preacher of love and justice. Harold Bloom, for example, emphasizes the strong influence of the language of the black church on Baldwin's style, pointing to its cadences and tone in Baldwin's use of religious language in his writings. While viewing Baldwin as a post-Christian writer, Bloom speaks of Baldwin's penchant for underscoring the rhetorical and aesthetic merit of black religious idioms, suggesting that it is these features of Baldwin's writings on religion that have most captured peoples' attention.[6]

Sondra O'Neale, another literary critic, acknowledges that much of the symbolism, language, and thematic calls for justice in Baldwin's essays are steeped in Christian ethics; nonetheless, she argues that his works do not reflect the traditional place of Christianity in black American literature. She further suggests that historically Baldwin should be seen "as the last black American writer to exploit as a major theme the black man's relationship with Christianity."[7] More recently, the literary theorist Douglas Field has concurred. He describes Baldwin as the last iconic writer in an African American literary tradition to have constructed narratives of black life against a backdrop of Christianity. For Field, the thematic shift in African American literature away from the influence of the black church also helps to explain why so many literary scholars have had little interest in exploring the role of black Christianity and the black church in Baldwin's life and work.[8]

These examples from Baldwin literary studies augment the complexity of issues related to any assessment of Baldwin's religiosity, which still awaits full analysis. As Michael Lynch, one of the few contemporary critics to focus on religion in Baldwin's writings, has repeatedly pointed out, "In spite of the profusion of biblical allusions and Christian symbols and themes throughout Baldwin's writing, the scholarship, aside from brief mention of the residual Christian content in his imagery . . . has offered no sustained treatment of his religious thought or theology."[9] Likewise, in confirming Bloom's sentiment, Field observes that although scholars acknowledge and identify a range of religious elements in Baldwin's writings, they continue to sustain more interest in his aesthetic, rhetorical, and stylistic use of the cadenced language of the church rather than in possible religious meanings. Field reminds us that "of nine full-length studies on Baldwin, only two books seriously consider him as a spiritual/religious writer;" for Field, this remains surprising given recent claims by scholars of a "return to religion" in contemporary literary theory.[10]

Whereas literary scholars continue to address religious themes and ideas in Baldwin's writings, very few religious scholars have seriously examined his canon with an eye toward assessing its religious content. One exception is Charles Hardy, whose recent study has brought renewed attention to Baldwin's Pentecostal background as central in understanding his radical racial rhetoric.[11] In *James Baldwin's God: Sex, Hope, and Crisis in Black Holiness Culture*, Hardy draws on literary and cultural theories to interpret the theological legacies of the black holiness culture often portrayed in Baldwin's writings.[12] Hardy's analysis is an important contribution to studies that show Baldwin representing forms of religious conflict as he depicts the sultry atmosphere of black urban church life in his work. Unlike most scholars, however, Hardy sustains attention to Baldwin's rejection of evangelical Christianity, its deity, and its symbolic world that vilified black people. In his explorations of Baldwin's rejection of Christianity and its deity as products of bad faith, Hardy provides insight into Baldwin's perception of these religious props as indelibly shaped by cultural constructions of whiteness, leading to black self-contempt and rejection of the body.

Following Hardy's lead, I examine further Baldwin's critique of institutionalized Christianity and the problematic links he drew between its symbolic worldview and the cultural values or religious practices that essentially established whiteness as representing normative humanity. A major focus of my discussion is the manner in which Baldwin addressed the ensuing self-hatred among blacks and the fear and hatred of blackness among whites. I also consider his juxtaposing both responses to a vision of love that emerged out of his expanded view of humanity. Thus, in my examination of Baldwin's complex relationship to religion, I am not interested in arguing for the strengths and weaknesses of the black holiness tradition, as Harding does, or in justifying Baldwin's personal theology as a legitimate call for Christianity to return to its roots. Rather, I seek to identify in Baldwin's critiques and visionary outlook elements of my conception of religious naturalism, which I believe is foreshadowed by Baldwin's call for African Americans to affirm their humanity and the integrity of their material bodies. As I discuss below, Baldwin believed the natural goodness of African Americans and their embodied existence was distorted by the reification of an abstract lie—whiteness—upheld by denigrating self-other differentiations. Furthermore, for Baldwin, one of the most pernicious forms of this structural differentiation was the religious doctrine demanding that impoverished, sinful black humans worship a white God.

The Tragic Position of Institutional Religion in Race Hatred

Baldwin's intellectual legacy includes compelling essays that feature his passionate views on religion, including his interpretation of the black holiness heritage that shaped his formative years. As a teenager Baldwin followed in his stepfather's footsteps and became a minister in the black holiness tradition; from the age of 14 until he was 17 he preached at the Fireside Pentecostal Church in Harlem. Of those teen years, Baldwin observes, "Those three years in the pulpit—I didn't realize it then—that is what turned me into a writer, really, dealing with all that anguish and that despair and that beauty."[13] Baldwin eventually rejected and moved beyond the Pentecostal tradition of his parents, but continued to address and symbolize in his writings its influence in American black urban life, as well as its limitations with regard to the psyches of its adherents. He would recall his youthful dismay in realizing that the "good news" contained in the leaflets he once dispersed to his classmates was in essence a set of harmful lies that aimed at instilling fear in the impressionable and the innocent. He sometimes described a Christian tradition that imposed upon worshippers a tyranny of beliefs grounded in rewards and punishments rather than full freedom. Furthermore, rather than upholding the naive notion of biblical inerrancy fostered by the holiness tradition of his youth, Baldwin asserted that the Bible itself had been written by white men in their favor. As he matured as a writer, Baldwin continued to develop a hermeneutics of suspicion toward institutional Christianity, which helped establish the increasingly popular view of Baldwin as antireligious. As Field notes, "After his vitriolic attacks on the church, notably in *The Fire Next Time* (1963) and *Tell Me How Long the Train's Been Gone* (1968), Baldwin was seen as a relentless social critic who had moved away from the institution of the church."[14]

In select writings, Baldwin targets both dominant white Christian culture and the black holiness tradition of his youth, which he saw as permeated by problematic ideological aspects of the former. In both systems of meaning, Baldwin identified a root problem, manifest in various ways and on different levels: systematic vilification of blackness. Key religious ideas functioned (either explicitly or implicitly) in a racist culture essentially to devalue black bodies as unworthy and inherently inferior to white ones, and they generated deeply embedded black self-loathing among many African Americans. In *To Crush a Serpent* (1987), one of his final published essays, Baldwin sums up a theme that he had addressed throughout many earlier ones: "Race and religion, it has been remarked, are fearfully entangled in the guts of this nation, so profoundly that to speak of the one is to conjure up the other. One cannot speak of sin without referring to blackness, and blackness stalks our history and our streets."[15] This passage may help to explain why Baldwin continued to be fascinated with religion even as he remained a harsh critic of its perceived limitations. I also think it provides some insight into Baldwin's ongoing interest in addressing religious imagery and ideas in essays and works of nonfiction. He appeared to have an acute awareness of the effects of religion as a system of meaning on the lives of individuals and of its capacity to offer an overall framework that adherents held in common.

I associate this aspect of Baldwin's focus on religion with Clifford Geertz's cultural anthropological approach to religion, where a primary objective is exploring how religion functions in the lives of individuals and communities. In his now classic essay "Religion as a Cultural System" first published in 1965, Geertz describes religion as a system of guidance, meaning, and authority in human affairs, and this definition of religion is one that scholars continue to borrow, adapt, and employ.[16] Geertz's theory of religion is primarily concerned with the interpretive sociology and anthropology of *meaning*, in the dual sense of its being both shaped by, and shaping, peoples' actions. In approaching religion as processes of meaning systems that are also accessible to outsiders, Geertz also focuses on what he calls the "thick description" of these meanings, or the collection of inscriptions rich and detailed enough to disentangle layers of structure of meanings in a socially constructed web of world formation. From this theoretical vantage point, one can fully appreciate Baldwin's fascination with religion and his specific focus on the role of religion within the dynamics of raced living.

In addressing the wider matrix of cultural meanings inhering in religious systems, and in showing how they both shape, and are shaped, by the behaviors of many black and white U.S. citizens, Baldwin targets the symbol *God*. For Baldwin, this symbol was a reified marker that posited whiteness as representative of aesthetic and moral truths and established whiteness as constitutive of normative humanity. Furthermore, whiteness was a social identity rooted in a god-complex, representing the dominant culture's desperate avoidance of its own limitations, as whites denied the beauty, value, and complex humanity of African Americans. Baldwin writes at length about the depth and pervasiveness of anti-blackness in American culture and its subtle embeddedness in religious mechanisms. In *The Fire Next Time*, Baldwin observes:

> Negroes in this country—and Negroes do not, strictly or legally speaking, exist in any other—are taught really to despise themselves from the moment their eyes open on the world. This world is white and they are black. White people hold the power, which means that they are superior to blacks (intrinsically, that is: God decreed it so), and the world has innumerable ways of making this difference known and felt and feared.[17]

In linking the notion of white supremacy with theistic belief and doctrinal certainty, Baldwin reveals why some cultural values entrenched in racial distortions appear as real, enduring, and authoritative truths. In the face of unrelenting racism and brutality, Baldwin thus saw religion as an obstacle to blacks' achieving authentic selfhood and integrity of being. In *To Crush a Serpent*, for example, Baldwin discusses the adverse psychological effects of those white Christian theological systems that invoked the curse of Ham to both justify slavery and devalue black subjectivities.[18] The rabid anti-blackness in such dangerous fabrications was alarming to Baldwin, who unmasked them as distortions of empirical truths. Although he was no longer under the sway of institutional religion, Baldwin felt and recognized its wide cultural effects on other blacks and many whites, and exposing the complex set of lies about black bodies and their essential depravity and inferiority became a primary goal of his humanistic agenda.

Even more troubling for Baldwin were the insidious psychological effects on blacks of paying homage to the Christian deity. In commenting on the paradoxical nature of worship in the God-intoxicated holiness tradition of his youth, he observes: "But God—and I felt this even then, so long ago, on that tremendous floor, unwilling—is white. And if His love was so great, and if He loved all His children, why were we, the black, cast down so far?"[19] Although he acknowledged that the black church (in all of its various structures) was a haven from blatant acts of racism, or a site of communal safety, Baldwin also saw its complicity with white supremacy, as blacks harbored fear and hatred of their own bodies and those that looked like theirs. He perceived a form of self-hatred embedded in his tradition's ritualistic fervor and rites of purification where, ironically, distraught religious adherents often denied themselves the healing, love, and pleasure they were entitled to experience: "And the passion with which we loved the Lord was a measure of how deeply we feared and distrusted, and, in the end, hated almost all strangers, always, and avoided and despised ourselves."[20] This awareness led Baldwin to another troubling insight: one unfortunate outcome of internalized anti-blackness was a lack of love in the black church. In *The Fire Next Time*, Baldwin muses, "I really mean that there was no love in the church," adding that it was a mask for "hatred and self-hatred and despair."[21] Baldwin experienced and witnessed the degree to which this self-hatred—extraordinarily moralistic in tone—was a guise for advancing anti-body, anti-sexual, xenophobic, and homophobic sentiments. Such anti-love fostered passivity and the repression of all that he and others experienced as naturally good, and it required the relinquishing of one's individuality.

Baldwin's Call for Freedom: Becoming One's Humanity

A careful reading of some of Baldwin's essays suggests that he infused his vision of racial equality with a fundamental search for authentic, dynamic selfhood. He viewed the national crisis with its unresolved race problem as a major opportunity for blacks and whites to begin embracing and experiencing life unimpeded by essentialist, facile views of humanity established by myriad institutions, including religious ones. Baldwin aptly describes this crisis in *The Fire Next Time* as an agonistic encounter between a white supremacist ideology intent on the systemic erasure of blacks' true humanity and an emerging black consciousness—one that he both finds within himself and associates with a collective black identity—that refuses to accept the external constructions imposed by white culture. As he observes, "the truth about the black man, as a historical entity and as a human being, *has* been hidden from him, deliberately and cruelly; the power of the white world is threatened whenever a black man refuses to accept the white world's definitions."[22] This is a crucial insight for Baldwin, revealing a theoretical strain in his racial discourse that relates to what some existentialists would identify as a perennial quest for authentic humanity.

As a philosophy of consciousness, existentialism posits human beings as self-conscious entities with the capacity to question and even doubt our existence. Added to this is the conviction that each individual finds him- or herself thrown into a world that is already given—this world provides the conditions of as well as the limits upon one's own journey toward self-understanding. Here, the Sartrean notion of forlornness, which implies thrownness, is helpful, for it suggests that we exist in a world not of our own making and indifferent to our concerns.[23] We are thrown into existence first without a predetermined nature, and only later do we construct our "nature" or "essence" through our actions. In advancing this perspective, Sartre rejects transcendent ideals (God, the Platonic forms, and so forth) often associated with the traditional metaphysical (specifically Christian) view, which posits that human beings have a given nature that determines both what we are and our ultimate purpose or value. He uses the example of a paper cutter to describe a traditional metaphysical view of human beings as artifacts, whose nature is tied to a preconceived essence and to a project outside of ourselves. While affirming the contrast between the world we are thrown into, which we cannot control, and the freedom we have to create ourselves, Sartre suggests that we must despair of receiving any hope of an external value or determination and simply restrict ourselves to what is under our own control.[24] With no predetermined meanings and no set values, humans exercise the freedom to create meanings as well as to create ourselves. In short, we bear full responsibility for such creations. In this Sartrean framework, as humans we are confronted with the responsibility of choosing our own nature and values; we also face the awesome responsibility of choosing human nature and values for all humans with our free choices.

While Baldwin's cultural critiques should not be conflated with Sartre's overall existential system or his universal pretensions, some interesting Sartrean themes are recognizable in his racial discourse. As noted above, Baldwin's writings reverberate with the truth of affirming life and embracing one's humanity in spite of the anguish that comes from existing in a world (or culture of values) that one has not created. This is a truth Baldwin lived while seeking a sense of authentic selfhood as he encountered racial distortions of his (and by extension, other blacks') humanity in the United States. In the beginning of "Nobody Knows My Name," he declares: "I left America because I doubted my ability to survive the fury of the color problem here. . . . I wanted to prevent myself from becoming *merely* a Negro; or, even, merely a Negro writer. I wanted to find out in what way the *specialness* of my experience could be made to connect me with other people instead of dividing me from them."[25] Here I imagine Baldwin as a scriptor of human possibilities, seeking an expansive view of the human capacity to relate and connect with others without being restricted by problematic racial constructs. With refreshing candor, he targeted white supremacy as a cultural value system that functioned to reduce and obscure his ability to connect with others (and with himself) on a more fundamental, existential level. In this system, his blackness—its symbolic resonance and its tactile materiality—became a source of alienation and disconnection based upon the disconcerting white gaze.

As Baldwin also discovered, another form of this alienation would be felt beyond American borders—in enlightened Europe. In the well-known essay "Stranger in the Village" (1953), Baldwin describes the anguish that besieged him while living in a tiny Swiss village. Reflecting on what it meant to be a stranger thrown into a raced world that he had not created, Baldwin observed that the people of the village could not be, from the point of view of power, strangers anywhere in the world. He writes about the children's response to him as an exotic rarity as they shout *Neger! Neger!* in the streets, oblivious to his reaction.[26] Notwithstanding the *saluts* and *bonsoirs* that Baldwin exchanges with his neighbors under the social convention of politeness, he sees in their eyes elements of paranoia and malevolence. In these encounters, Baldwin understood (or grasped) his identity as "the black" in personal and passionate terms. Notably, for Baldwin this encounter with self was not a result of a disembodied, detached abstraction, but rather of deep involvement in the concreteness and full materiality of life. Existing authentically required his immersion in the richness of experience, gathering whatever insights and knowledge it brought to him. His experience in the Swiss village led him to reflect on the European roots of white racism and its later appearance in the United States: There is no European innocence, and the ideas on which American beliefs are based originated in Europe. He writes, "For this village brings home to me this fact: that there was a day, and not really a very distant day, when Americans were scarcely Americans at all but discontented Europeans, facing a great unconquered continent and strolling, say, into a marketplace and seeing black men for the first time."[27] The very visibility of blackness that Baldwin alludes to—the sight of black skin—measures the importance of materiality in his racial discourse.

Baldwin's European experiences and travels shaped his conviction that once one finds oneself in another cultural setting, one is forced to examine one's own culture. In the early 1960s, he returned to North America to take part in the civil rights movement, compelled by a sense of urgency to address the racial unrest in the nation. Traveling throughout the South provided him with more material for reflecting systematically on the quandaries of affirming blackness amid the horrors of U.S. racial struggles. Set within the context of Baldwin's thoughts on raced living, Sartre's universalizing tendencies are recast to elevate the crucial social, cultural, and political implications of existentialist truths in black life. In the essay "The White Problem," for instance, Baldwin states that as a youth he had been seduced by American democratic ideals, which impressed upon the nation's denizens the dream of authentic selfhood. He sardonically sketches the immediate, felt experience of white racism for blacks as that of being thrown into an alien universe wholly indifferent to one's concerns. Moreover, he observes, within the construction of raced living, African Americans are not given the liberty of claiming the source of their existence; they also lack access to any external source of value and determination, as the white God is useless. At this juncture, Baldwin shows his genius in characterizing the sense of exile, dread, and revolt against despair in such an irrational universe. He encourages blacks to name and embrace their humanity, asserting "that whatever it is you want, what you want, at bottom, must be to *become yourself*: there is nothing else to want."[28]

In "The White Problem," a speech delivered in May 1964, Baldwin is addressing the urgency of the crisis in Birmingham, Alabama and the irony of celebrating one hundred years of "Negro freedom," as he evokes the issue of human identity and authentic freedom. In this address, Baldwin mentions the Klan bombing of the 16th Street Baptist Church—a meeting place for civil rights leaders and a site of activism—in Birmingham on September 15, 1963, that left four young black girls dead and many other people injured. Using the brutality of white racism (for example, the various, often unresolved, bombings occurring in Birmingham that symbolize southern white culture's resistance to blacks' essential act of self-determination) as a backdrop, Baldwin utters an important lesson: there is a fundamental task before all human beings, and this is the ongoing creation of oneself. In my idiom, it is becoming one's humanity. Evoking the Nietzschean sentiment of "descend[ing] deeper than I have ever before descended,"[29] Baldwin alludes to the radical alterity that structures human identity: "The truth, forever, for everyone, is that one is a stranger to oneself, and that one must deal with this stranger day in and day out—that one, in fact, is forced to create, as distinct from invent, oneself."[30] Baldwin's words conjure up the Sartrean notion that our subjectivity is the starting point for understanding human freedom. Affirming life is akin to exercising that freedom.

Not one to flinch from embracing life's tragic dimensions, Baldwin often spoke of having the courage and determination not to let death and its finality deter us from choosing life, as this passage from *The Fire Next Time* reflects:

> Life is tragic simply because the earth turns and the sun inexorably rises and sets, and one day, for each of us, the sun will go down for the last, last time. Perhaps the whole root of our trouble, the human trouble, is that we will sacrifice all the beauty of our lives, will imprison ourselves in totems, taboos, crosses, blood sacrifices, steeples, mosques, races, armies, flags, nations, in order to deny the fact of death, which is the only fact we have. It seems to me that one ought to rejoice in the *fact* of death—ought to decide, indeed, to *earn* one's death by confronting with passion the conundrum of life. One is responsible to life: It is the small beacon in that terrifying darkness from which we come and to which we shall return. One must negotiate this passage as nobly as possible, for the sake of those who come after us.[31]

In light of the irrefutable fact of death, Baldwin forges the values of claiming one's humanity and affirming life. The individualization process involved in enacting one's humanity is a basic affirmation that one can actualize oneself and become what one desires; as Baldwin asserts, it is essentially saying yes to life. By the same token, Baldwin maintains that the wider identity crisis of the nation, which had its inception at the black slave's auction block, lies in the fact that it has prohibited its black denizens this opportunity: "Now, in this country this inability to say yes to life is part of our dilemma, which could become a tragic one."[32]

For Baldwin, materiality counts, and as a consequence, the material, embodied human being must be appreciated, valued, and saved from destructive forces. In affirming this truth, he opposes the holiness tradition of his youth that focused on an individual's immaterial soul as the proper object of redemption. Recognizing the destructive effects of white racism on the black humanity he both embodied and saw around him, Baldwin underscored black bodies as centers of value, whose worth should not be overshadowed by the power of any institution—religious or otherwise. In a very expressive passage in *The Fire Next Time*, Baldwin shared his first awakening to this crucial insight:

> I was even lonelier and more vulnerable than I had been before. And the blood of the Lamb had not cleansed me in any way whatever. I was just as black as I had been the day that I was born. Therefore, when I faced the congregation, it began to take all the strength I had not to stammer, not to curse, not to tell them to throw away their Bibles and get off their knees and go home and organize, for example, a rent strike. When I watched all the children, their copper, brown, and beige faces staring up at me as I taught Sunday school, I felt that I was committing a crime in talking about the gentle Jesus, in telling them to reconcile themselves to their misery on earth in order to gain the crown of eternal life. Were only Negroes to gain this crown? Was Heaven, then, to be merely another ghetto?[33]

Baldwin's discourse signals a form of existential revolt, resisting, among other things, the dangerous myth of white superiority with its requisite demands for silent, black suffering and passive compliance with unjust white structures. Yet, while Baldwin rejects a model of religious victimology for blacks within North American culture, he also acknowledges that suffering is an aspect of living; it is an integral component of becoming human in the quest for self-understanding. His sense of this experience approaches the existential notion of ontological despair associated with fully facing the structure of experience, which often generates a complex of feelings: anxiety, pain, insecurity, and so forth. For existentialists, this uniquely human capacity becomes manifest in the course of our lives because it is a rational reaction to the painful, unpredictable world that assails us. It is a commonsense response to the perception that the universe appears indifferent, often seemingly hostile to us, that we are mere specks of dust in a complex, whirling, expanding universe. Within this context, the existential revolter recognizes the anguish of becoming human, of embracing one's humanity and not simply existing as an object that others can manipulate and control. In Sartrean terms, it is choosing *etre-pour-soi* (being-for-itself) and refusing to rest in *etre-en-soi* (being-in-itself).[34] Thus, we hear Baldwin assert:

> I do not mean to be sentimental about suffering—enough is certainly as good as a feast—but people who cannot suffer can never grow up, can never discover who they are. That man who is forced each day to snatch his manhood, his identity, out of the fire of human cruelty that rages to destroy it knows, if he survives his effort, and even if he does not survive it, something about himself and human life that no school on earth—and, indeed, no church—can teach. He achieves his own authority, and that is unshakeable.[35]

Baldwin's reminder in the above passage is clear: the efforts involved in actively revolting against the impositions of an unjust cultural system are inextricably connected to self-knowledge and to affirming one's valuable humanity. In short, for Baldwin, a basic task required of every African American is claiming her or his humanity—in essence, this means both acquiring authentic self-knowledge and affirming life. Additionally, he is quick to note that the unavoidable form of suffering entailed in pursuing this fundamental task should not be confused with a benign passivity to the unjust, systemic forms of exploitation found in our constructed societies. Take, for example, Baldwin's use of the phrase *improbable aristocrats* to describe young black men and women across the South who faced, with nonviolent resistance, white mobs protesting their entrance into public schools and universities. For Baldwin, these forms of protest were heroic acts of self-determination by youth claiming their humanity. "In hewing over the mountain of white supremacy," Baldwin felt they were achieving their distinctiveness—"the stone of their individuality."[36] This general idea becomes an integral part of Baldwin's moral vision as he defines the history of African Americans as decisively shaped by their "endless struggle" for "human identity" in the context of "death and humiliation."[37]

Freedom from Race Hatred and Becoming One's Humanity

In the 1963 essay "We Can Change the Country," Baldwin describes a key issue for African Americans intent on embracing their authentic humanity: the eradication of self-hatred, or the internalized racism that resulted from living under what Du Bois had called "the veil." Addressing the anti-black fervor of dominant white culture, Baldwin passionately states: "It is the American Republic—repeat, the American Republic—which created something which they call a 'nigger.' They created it out of necessities of their own."[38] As stated earlier, Baldwin believed the tumultuous events inaugurated by the civil rights movement were predictable because the nation was facing an identity crisis—and this crisis hinged on the fact that he and many other African Americans were both unmasking and denouncing the great lie. As a prototypical voice of collective black identity, Baldwin states that he is not a "nigger" and had never been one. In a critical positioning of reclaiming his true humanity, Baldwin poses a crucial question to the American Republic: "Why do you need a 'nigger' in the first place, and what are you going to do about him now that he's moved out of his place? Because I am not what you said I was. And if my place, as it turns out, is not my place, then you are not what you said you were, and where's your place?"[39]

Baldwin continues this theme in another piece, "My Dungeon Shook: Letter to My Nephew on the One Hundredth Anniversary of the Emancipation," one of the two essays that comprise *The Fire Next Time*. In this passionate missive, Baldwin describes with unrelenting, brutal honesty the America his young nephew James has inherited, and the birthright assigned to the young black male and countless others like him. For Baldwin, the younger James becomes a symbol for all gifted black youth who represent a new ideal, or a movement beyond the destructive forces of the past that have kept certain minds imprisoned with self-hatred. He writes: "You can only be destroyed by believing that you really are what the white world calls a *nigger*."[40] Baldwin also holds that certain details and symbols in James' young life were deliberately constructed to make him believe what white people say about him.

Baldwin astutely describes the psychological dynamics operating in the construction of whiteness in the United States; these are subjectivities that rely on the perceived inferiority of blacks in order to secure their own white identities as normatively human. He later addressed this idea succinctly in a dialogue with Nikki Giovanni, when observing that "white people invented black people to give white people identity."[41] In light of this theme, Baldwin sketches a terrifying image of a dominant white culture that refuses to see its complicity in creating and sustaining others' denigration. In describing this cultural violence, in *The Fire Next Time* Baldwin says, "they have destroyed and are destroying hundreds of thousands of lives and do not know it and do not want to know it."[42] This naivety, Baldwin declares, is the worst type of innocence, as it refuses to see its own limitations and its destructive effects on others. In this case, Baldwin takes the typical abstract, oppositional logic that helps to make sense of mutually interdependent meanings (white/black, rich/poor, good/bad) and recasts them to unveil the skewed power dynamics of language that literally affect the material lives of human bodies.

Baldwin points to the violence inherent in an innocence that dictates that certain bodies (black ones) "be born under conditions not very far removed from those described by Charles Dickens in the London of more than a hundred years ago."[43] Here, as elsewhere, Baldwin does not flinch from describing blackness as a material reality that whites truly abhor, as he tells his nephew, "You were born where you were born and faced the future that you faced because you were black and *for no other reason*."[44] As did Anna Julia Cooper and W. E. B. Du Bois in their respective cultural critiques, Baldwin also attends to the impoverished cultural standards associated with blackness, suggesting that his nephew is not expected to aspire to excellence, but "to make peace with mediocrity."[45] With a penetrating insight that went to the heart of race and identity in the United States during his day, Baldwin saw that the individual success of young blacks like his nephew could not be divorced from the larger ontological issue of blacks and whites grasping their freedom together—in essence, this meant collectively embracing their common humanity.

Achieving Our Humanity: Embracing Freedom and Loving One Another

Baldwin's view of human freedom led him to indict the construction of whiteness and its concomitant system of racism in the United States. Both, he contended, aided in denying the common humanity that all shared, and fostered myriad forms of alienation and hatred among individuals and groups. This vision inspired his participation in the civil rights movement, which he believed was a major opportunity for participants to help redeem a nation that had failed repeatedly to enact its principles of freedom and liberty. The call for freedom that Baldwin featured again and again, however, is one that underscores a paradoxical insight: only black freedom will make white freedom possible. For Baldwin this truth was anchored in the essential quest that every human being must undertake: seeking self-knowledge and living authentically.

He described African Americans in the nation as increasingly aware that their freedom hinged on their ability to wrestle back from the hands of white imperialism their claim to their full humanity: blacks must struggle ceaselessly against impoverished, externalized views of their humanity and reclaim the more authentic sense of themselves as powerful, dignified, valued entities. Until this movement occurred, the nation would not see the fullness of freedom extolled in the lofty words of its founding documents or in its various emancipation movements. Achieving full freedom for the citizens of the nation, however, would not be merely a matter of conversion of black's subjective awareness; it would also require the destruction of unjust power structures built on the erroneous notion of white superiority. Baldwin scholar Clarence Hardy references an interesting conversation Baldwin had with Reinhold Niebuhr, in which Baldwin observes the irony of enslaved people being the only hope of the country. For Baldwin, black people are the only hope because their suffering has helped them discover what they really live by, whereas most white Americans are preoccupied with a crass consumerism, worrying more about Coca-Cola than about the issues of social justice.[46]

In his 1964 essay "What Price Freedom?" Baldwin is very clear that the struggle toward freedom that whites must undertake is not identical to the one that must be undertaken by blacks, precisely because there is such a fundamental lack of self-knowledge on the part of whites. Another way of articulating this problem is to raise a crucial question: What lies behind white culture's presumption of superiority? To return for a moment to the existential motif of seeking one's authentic humanity, Baldwin's general answer references the dangerous fabrications of self-deception that can drive individuals and even nations to inauthentic existence. In another essay, "Nothing Personal," (1964), he observes:

> It has always been much easier (because it has always seemed much safer), to give a name to the evil without than to locate the terror within. And yet, the terror within is far truer and far more powerful than any of our labels: the labels change, the terror is constant. And this terror has something to do with that irreducible gap between the self one invents—the self one takes oneself as being, which is, however, and by definition, a provisional self—and the undiscoverable self which always has the power to blow the provisional self to bits. It is perfectly possible—indeed, it is far from uncommon—to go to bed one night, or wake up one morning, or simply walk through a door one has known all one's life, and discover, between inhaling and exhaling, that the self one has sewn together with such effort is all dirty rags, is unusable, is gone: and out of what raw material will one build a self again? The lives of men—and, therefore, of nations—to an extent literally unimaginable, depend on how vividly this question lives in the mind.[47]

Whites' relinquishing of their self-deception, or sense of superiority over blacks, becomes an essential movement toward authentic selfhood and existence. Thus, in the midst of this bold assumption, Baldwin eloquently suggests that until white Americans can take him—a black man—in their arms, there will be no freedom or comfort of being. If America's success lies in the capacity for all of its denizens to be free, then the price for such freedom is a basic, radical transformation of human relations within raced living. In short, for whites, it involves embracing the perceived otherness of blackness as an essential part of their own humanity. As he states it, this is "the price a white woman, man, boy, and girl will have to pay in themselves before they look on me as another human being. This metamorphosis is what we are driving toward, because without that we will perish—indeed, we are almost perishing now."[48]

These observations of Baldwin converge with a basic aspect of my theory of sacred humanity: human beings as value-laden organisms fundamentally coming to terms with life, or making sense of their existence, in relationship with others. Furthermore, in making a claim on life within our constructed worlds of meaning, we both envision and make possible new forms of relationality. This insight converges with Baldwin's insistence on a rich, embodied form of human love that inspired and challenged his contemporaries to conceive and hope beyond what seemed immediate and obvious. To reach this goal, he believed white Americans had to confront and resist the great lie that had been constructed to justify the historical phenomenon of slavery, which his contemporaries continued to perpetuate: the cultural construction of blacks' inferiority and their less-then human nature.

As referenced above, Baldwin saw African Americans reclaiming and loving their blackness as naturally good, clinging to their love of life, and continuing to survive against the greatest odds. In describing the psychology of embodying one's blackness, Baldwin observes:

> It is hard to be black, and therefore officially, and lethally, despised.
> It is harder than that to despise so many of the people who think of themselves as white, before whose blindness you present the obligatory historical grin.
>   And it is harder than that, out of this devastation—Ezekiel's valley: "Oh Lord, can these bones live?"—to trust life, and to live a life, to love, and be loved.[49]

Thus, while Baldwin often describes and acknowledges the hatred he and other blacks feel toward whites in experiencing their gaze of otherness, he also asserts that the redemption of our common humanity requires a radical form of embracing the other. For Baldwin, this complex task is inextricably tied to the theme of love, which he infuses into the harrowing, ongoing account of racism and its effects on all U.S. denizens. To his black comrades, Baldwin declares: "There is no reason for you to try to become like white people and there is no basis whatever for their impertinent assumption that *they* must accept *you*. The really terrible thing, old buddy, is that *you* must accept *them*. And I mean that very seriously. You must accept them and accept them with love. For these innocent people have no other hope."[50] Here one finds Baldwin articulating, admittedly in a very different voice, Cooper's vision of "one and all" with the impassioned insistence that liberation for the country cannot happen until both black and white people are liberated from the dominant cultural mythos that has sustained the nation's identity for several centuries: an inferior black humanity.

Baldwin often creatively sketches the varied levels of estrangement that occur between whites and blacks in a race-infused world by using very powerful metaphors. Among these is the "bastard" metaphor, which critics suggest is a key one for understanding Baldwin's desire to capture the displaced and exilic status of black American existence. Part of this exilic experience, Baldwin suggests, is white Americans' denial of literal familial kinship with blacks. As he observed in an interview with James Mossman, "The great dilemma of being a white American precisely is that they deny their only kinship."[51] His race-conscious rhetoric often focuses on the hypocrisy of white Christians invested in preserving a white identity that refused to accept its moral connection and biological kinship with African Americans.

Baldwin's use of the bastard metaphor has elicited a range of critical responses, from Cornel West's distrust of a perceived apolitical individualism to Charles Hardy's declaration that Baldwin was poignantly seeking recognition from whites.[52] However, I prefer to see it as a deeper expression of Baldwin's form of communal ontology that recognizes a common humanity constitutive of our biotic materiality, to which various identity markers are attached. With the bastard motif, Baldwin underscored impoverished views of humanity kept in place by polarized, binary constructions (for example, white / black, insider / outsider, superiority / inferiority, the saved / the damned, heterosexual-normal / homosexual-depraved). In my reading, Baldwin's bastard metaphor alerts readers to his aspirations toward acquiring ontological wholeness both for himself and others. Later in his life, while reflecting on his sojourns in Europe, and implicitly conjoining the singular with the collective, Baldwin inscribed a type of existence for black Americans that could at best be described, pathetically, as nonessential and marginal. In "Autobiographical Notes" from *Notes of a Native Son*, Baldwin asserts:

> I know, in any case, that the most crucial time in my own development came when I was forced to recognize that I was a kind of bastard of the West; when I followed the line of my past I did not find myself in Europe but in Africa. And this meant that in some subtle way, in a really profound way, I brought to Shakespeare, Bach, Rembrandt, to the stones of Paris, to the cathedral at Chartres, and to the Empire State Building, a special attitude. These were not really my creations, they did not contain my history; I might search in them in vain forever for any reflection of myself. I was an interloper; this was not my heritage.[53]

The cultural resonance of Baldwin's bastard metaphor is noteworthy here. The cultural artifacts he encounters that purportedly symbolize the best of human aspirations, desires, hopes, and creativity do not reflect his contributions as an African American. With sobering awareness, his sense of illegitimacy is heightened when he realizes that in this Euro-American cultural lineage, he was essentially being confronted with prevailing configurations of the normative human: an ideology of whiteness. With a critical awareness of experiencing oneself, one's people, one's culture as not quite genuine—as irregular, inferior, or of dubious origin—Baldwin speaks of cultivating a "special attitude," a "special place in this scheme."[54] While not denying the reality of cultural, historical forces, Baldwin also declares that humans are always so much more than what our cultural markers claim for us. As he realizes, "I had to claim my birthright. I am what time, circumstance, history, have made of me, certainly, but I am, also, much more than that. So are we all."[55]

This passage helps underscore the ontological implications implicit in Baldwin's critical discourse. Claiming one's heritage is part of a more complex process of actualizing oneself as one relates to others, aspiring to achieve and experience one's humanity without falling prey to the damaging effects of a binary system that demarcates some humans as more, others as less. Furthermore, Baldwin insisted on honoring materiality, corporeality, and physical realities, asserting again and again that black and white Americans are blood relatives. What his contemporaries often perceived as a racial problem essentially masked a more fundamental problem: forgetfulness of our common humanity. As he declares in *No Name in the Street*: "The problem is rooted in the question of how one treats one's flesh and blood, especially one's children. The blacks are the despised and slaughtered children of the great Western house—nameless and unnamable bastards."[56]

Baldwin's insistence that whites see themselves in blacks (and *as black*) supports the basic thrust of my religious naturalism, which emphasizes the deep genetic homology structuring all life forms—what I earlier described as human beings' interconnectedness with one another and with all natural organisms. As Baldwin emphatically states at one point: "It is so simple a fact and one that is so hard, apparently, to grasp: *Whoever debases others is debasing himself.*"[57] Furthermore, Baldwin associates the term *love* with this critical awareness of our common humanity. Akin to the existential mode of being, love for Baldwin describes a state of being one affirms again and again in the process of choosing to enact one's authentic humanity. Note Baldwin's words: "Love takes off the masks that we fear we cannot live without and know we cannot live within. I use the word 'love' here not merely in the personal sense but as a state of being, or a state of grace—not in the infantile American sense of being made happy but in the tough universal sense of quest and daring and growth."[58]

What I am suggesting is that Baldwin's notion of love has deep theoretical and cultural significance. Amid the violent forms of alienation caused by problematic racial distinctions, he articulates a moral vision that imbues traditional religious terms with fresh, expanded meanings. For example, Baldwin rejects the traditional otherworldly, eschatological discourse of fear and damnation featured in holiness traditions, replacing it with an emphasis on the concrete dynamics of living here and now. For him, love is "something active, more like a fire, like a wind," not an empty abstraction pointing to a passive stance before some authorial figure outside of oneself.[59] Likewise, salvation is that which we must do to save one another; the most crucial aspect of salvation for Baldwin is its rootedness in human actions and efforts. The contingencies of life and the concreteness of human experiences require redemptive actions from humans themselves. This view evokes the Sartrean notion of intersubjectivity: recognizing the humanity of the other before oneself confronts one's subjectivity in the most immediate way, both limiting and enabling what one could possibly choose in any given context. As Baldwin asserts, "Salvation does not divide. Salvation connects, so that one sees oneself in others and others in oneself. It is not the exclusive property of any dogma, creed, or church. It keeps the channel open between oneself and however one wishes to name That which is greater than oneself."[60]

Baldwin reiterated this theme in a speech he gave in San Francisco in October 1960. Addressing the writer's role in American life, Baldwin shares a moral vision that celebrates the potential of newly formed human relationships to create and sustain new possibilities for Americans. In his thinking, humans displace the traditional God and enact transformation in their lives, redeeming themselves from impoverished, erroneous views of their shared humanity. For example, after insisting on necessary changes to the dominant configuration of raced living in America, Baldwin ends the speech with the following words about America's future: "It will not be transformed by an act of God, but by all of us, by you and me. I don't believe any longer that we can afford to say that it is entirely out of our hands. We made the world we're living in and we have to make it over."[61] As suggested earlier, in traditional African American religiosity, the divine concept is rooted in a metaphysical system that pits a supernatural deity over against sinful humans. Here one sees Baldwin displacing this traditional supernaturalism, exchanging the external deity beyond nature for the power of love expressed in embodied, material human relationships.

For Baldwin, human beings save one another. As D. Quentin Miller has suggested, one can see Baldwin moving from the ultimate expression of external authority—God—to the broader community, collectively and individually.[62] In doing so, his anti-transcendental discourse hints at my fuller notion of sacred humanity. Baldwin's divine other becomes value-laden humans whose actions with and aspirations for one another constitute their sacrality. Here we cherish the material, concrete human as a center of value. In keeping with my concept of sacred humanity, Baldwin's view of humanity offers an acute awareness of an appreciable world of ideal values that awaits us: what we can become, and what we wish to be depends on how we act in the here and now. In the most immediate sense, this construction of humanity is dependent on radical acts of love—the embracing of otherness within oneself and as oneself. As Baldwin eloquently asserts in *The Fire Next Time*, "we, with love, shall force our [white] brothers to see themselves as they are, to cease fleeing from reality, and begin to change it. ... [W]e can make America what America must become."[63]

Conclusion: Toward an African American Religious Naturalism

> And our great "problem" after all is to be solved not by brooding over it, and orating about it, but by *living into it*.
>
> —ANNA JULIA COOPER, "What Are We Worth?"

While addressing the problematics of raced living in the United States, Anna Julia Cooper, W. E. B. Du Bois, and James Baldwin posed tacit yet important questions that often come to the fore in religious discourse. These are questions of hope and aspiration, which include: What if? Why not? Could it be? More specifically, in challenging impoverished (albeit influential) views of African Americans during the early to mid–twentieth century, these iconic figures advocated that all Americans at least attend to these questions, as the untenable alternative is ceasing to use human potential toward the construction of more benevolent, just worlds. What those worlds eventually turn out to be depends very much on which values subsequent generations of Americans choose for structuring and sustaining what we conceive of as our humanity. With the naturalistic perspectives of this study, I have aspired to participate in this ongoing humanistic task. The African American religious naturalism I endorse encourages a new generation of dreamers to move beyond past, deficient constructions of our humanity and imagine new possibilities that emphasize our lived experience as embodied, value-laden, and social organisms. It emphasizes our common humanity, what you and I share, which is irreducibly sacred and constitutive of deep, inextricable connection. This is translatable as our capacity to be in authentic relation with the other. Furthermore, as a new religious ideal, the concept of sacred humanity ennobles and dignifies new images of ourselves, creatively inscribed onto the tissues, bones, and liquids of which we are constituted.

Establishing sacred humanity within the framework of religious naturalism has also helped me advance in a radically different way a thematic concern of traditional African American religiosity, namely, the intrinsic value of black humanity. Furthermore, in tracing aspects of this religious ideal in the writings of Cooper, Du Bois, and Baldwin, I have presented a trajectory of black intellectualism that contributes to an emerging African American religious naturalism. As suggested earlier, these iconic figures' critiques of white supremacy at various historical junctures are more than social critiques; aspects of their ideas also foreshadow, converge with, and even illuminate the fuller conceptual insights I associate with the principle of sacred humanity.

This model of religious naturalism points to a tenacious refusal of African Americans (and other human beings) to reduce our various actions to mere brute existence or to see our lives in terms of determinist forces and mechanistic explanations of cause and effect. I associate this impulse with our ability to reflect upon the past, to assess the present, and, inevitably, to consider the future. In short, the African American religious naturalism I introduce here symbolically represents what the human individual or group might creatively accomplish with an expanded concept of our humanity; it may also serve as a guide to behavior. Here I invoke Whitehead's view of religiosity as "the vision of something which stands beyond, behind, and within, the passing flux of immediate things; something which is real, and yet waiting to be realized; something which is a remote possibility, and yet the greatest of present facts; something that gives meaning to all that passes, and yet eludes apprehension."[1]

This religious quality has been variously expressed as the desire to experience a profound intimacy with others, or perhaps to construct "worlds" of meaningful relations, or, sometimes, as the desire to discover fuller dimensions of reality, beyond what appears obvious. In any case, the question of whether there may be the possibility of something more or some positivity (however that is conceived) beyond what we currently experience has been (and continues to be) a persistently religious one. In light of these assumptions, I end this study with some brief reflections on the major themes I have been developing throughout the various chapters. Specifically, I summarize some key aspects of this model of African American religious naturalism, highlight important implications, and offer a sense of its potential value within both African American life and U.S. culture.

Proper Focus on Sacred Human Beings: Artful, Material Organisms

My model of African American religious naturalism emerges out of a critical awareness that religiosity is not necessarily centered in any specific tradition; rather, it can be a mode of reflecting on, experiencing, and envisioning one's relationality with all that is. Here, I evoke the views of Peter Van Ness, who writes, "the spiritual dimension of life is the embodied task of realizing one's truest self in the context of reality apprehended as a cosmic totality. It is the quest for attaining an optimal relationship between what one truly is and everything that is."[2] Consequently, a fuller emergence of this African American religious naturalism is possible if, and only if, we continue to keep our focus on artful, material human organisms, or on the efforts of sacred humanity. Within the context of African American life and culture, this means that any truths we are ever going to discover, and any meanings in life we will uncover, are revealed to us through our own efforts as natural beings. This religious view expressly rejects any suggestion of the supernatural—there is nothing here that transcends the natural world. Donald Crosby provides an elegant summary of the prominent status of nature in religious naturalism:

> Nature requires no explanation beyond itself. It always has existed and always will exist in some shape or form. Its constituents, principles, laws, and relations are the sole reality. This reality takes on new traits and possibilities as it evolves inexorably through time. Human beings are integral parts of nature, and they are natural beings through and through. They, like all living beings, are outcomes of biological evolution. They are embodied beings whose mental or spiritual aspect is not something separate from their bodies but a function of their bodily nature. There is no realm of the supernatural and no supernatural being or beings residing in such a realm.[3]

As Cooper intimated during her lifetime, nature itself can become the focal point for assessing our human desires, dreams, and possibilities—for assessing what can emerge from the past. However, a century removed from Cooper's Romanticism and her unique approach to naturalistic imagery, I now envision a religious naturalism that requires African Americans to take seriously the idea of emergence in scientific studies. More specifically, this African American religious naturalism compels African Americans to reflect meaningfully on the emergence of matter, and especially of life, from the Big Bang forward, promoting an understanding of myriad nature as complex processes of becoming. Its theoretical appeal is the fundamental conception of human beings as natural processes intrinsically connected to other natural processes. This insight helps to blur the arbitrary ontological lines that human animals have erected between ourselves and other species and natural processes. The advances of science, through both biology and physics, have served to demonstrate not only how closely linked we are with nature, but that we humans are simply one branch of a seemingly endless natural cosmos. Furthermore, this naturalistic turn in black religiosity accentuates a fuller sense of biotic integrity: newer forms of embodied relationality that enables vital flourishing among all sentient entities compel us. Our religious sensibilities dictate human engagement with diverse processes of life. With these assumptions, African American religious scriptors advance the image of humanity as value-laden organisms within community—as an evolving, multileveled network of interdependent beings, as Cooper asserted with her multifaceted Romantic vision.

African American Religious Naturalism and Experiences of Otherness

I suggested earlier that human beings are specific biotic entities emerging from evolutionary processes. A major implication of this claim is that the evolutionary narrative propels humans' efforts to create meaning and purpose here, and, I now add, to aspire toward myriad forms of ethical praxis.[4] As value-laden organisms, human animals are capable of ethical discourse, which inspires some of us to challenge viral constructions of "isms" rooted in problematic and alienating self-other differentiations, especially those racially constructed ones that Cooper, Du Bois, and Baldwin targeted. This African American religious naturalism thus invites contemporaries to reflect further on Du Bois's insights regarding the existential matrix constituting the lived realities of humans. This implies a central focus on the conception of our humanity as social beings who enter into relations with perceived others—a focus that also bears in mind the rhetorical richness of Baldwin's racial discourse. For example, the concept of sacred humanity absorbs Baldwin's historical insights regarding the notion of blackness as a form of otherness in a cultural formation that reifies whiteness, affirming his sense that full liberation for all Americans requires a rejection of the dualistic, binary structures that support such problematic views of otherness. As Baldwin contended, embracing our full humanity requires Americans to bring our full attention to important social, psychological, and existential insights that aid in myriad, radical forms of transformation. The concept of sacred humanity functions in the contemporary era to advance these claims; it is also in harmony with Latina feminist philosopher Ofelia Schutte's determination that the other is not only "that person occupying the space of the subaltern in the culturally asymmetrical power relation, but also those elements or dimensions of the self that unsettle or decenter the ego's dominant, self-enclosed, territorialized identity."[5]

This principle of sacred humanity also acknowledges humans' radical historicity and the inevitability of encounters with otherness, which is another way of accentuating crucial intersubjective experiences in which the human subject comes face to face with an-other reality. Sacred humanity assumes precognitive, extralinguistic experiences from which arise the conviction that one is not alone. Furthermore, through an awareness of our material, concrete embodiment and perceived relatedness, we may begin to envision what might lie beyond our self-perceptions and thoughts. As we encounter others and ourselves in a host of ways, we are guided by an interpretive mandate, which compels us to derive meaning, purpose, and value amid our efforts to recognize and honor otherness. In this context, the other may be identified with the many worlds that we inhabit, that is, the organic or natural systems that surround us; the other may also connote constructed and symbolic worlds of ideas and thoughts, the physical, constructed world of social institutions, and the internal, psychological realms that also help to configure our sense of selfhood. One direct implication is that we humans ought always to be expected to invent, create, or construct viable worlds of meaning and significance. Here the Heideggerian notion of truth as "revelatory" is implied, in which a partial, open-ended, and tentative epistemology will always accompany one's interpretive practices. In remaining open to our experiences of alterity or otherness, human animals are constantly transformed, finding meaning, purpose, and quality in our existence as sacred humans, or as *homo religious*.

Sacred Humanity, Relationality, and Religious Valuing

As Cooper and Baldwin showed during their lifetimes, within the context of certain American racial configurations that have persistently denied blacks our full humanity, any view of our humanity as a solely individualistic phenomenon is rejected—some type of communal ontology is implied. With the contemporary religious naturalism that I advance, African Americans continually remind ourselves—and all denizens of the country who might perceive and experience themselves as unified, separate entities—that every "I" inevitably confronts on a daily basis the facticity, experiences, thoughts, wishes, and desires of other life forms and subjectivities. Such is the lived experience of sacred humanity. Here the "I" is not even meaningful without the context, or other, that allows this "I" to be. In other words, this form of religious valuing reinforces the anthropological and sociological insights that we are social beings who necessarily interact and derive profound meaning from our relations with others. With the concept of sacred humanity, we are essentially celebrating a relational self that can resist solipsistic tendencies and egoistic impulses: there is no isolated self that stands over against the fields of interaction. Put another way, there is no wholly private self or final line between interiority and exteriority—we always include the other, even when acting to exclude it. The self is constitutionally relational and inevitably entangled in temporal becoming. As expressed earlier, the sacred humanity concept entails religious valuing that shows humans as primarily constituted and enhanced by our efforts to interpret, make sense of, symbolize, and assess our relations with otherness.

My further suggestion is that the form of religious valuing associated with the idea of the sacredness of human beings becomes one precondition for conceiving particular notions of communal moral reasoning, for it is only through an acceptance of one's material, concrete embodiment and perceived relatedness that one begins envisioning (or is even challenged to think of) what may lie beyond one's own self-perceptions and thoughts. Hence, it is not surprising that historically, religious systems have sought to provide integrative frameworks of a perceived whole, often in transhistorical, objective, or universal terms. The various cosmologies, metaphysics, and value systems emerging from the world's religions show a persistent human propensity to construct worldviews that express something more, beyond the commonsense knowledge and restrictions of empirical data.

These assumptions lead me to suggest that when we think about religious valuing in humans, we are acknowledging at least minimally a fundamental human propensity toward life that features distinctive cognitive and emotive elements. Uniting cognition and affectivity, viewing them as inseparable elements of religious valuing, departs from empiricist approaches that focus exclusively on religious knowledge. It is akin to Crosby's suggestion that religious naturalism's concept of nature "does not rest solely on the evidence of the five senses but assumes the critical relevance of other types of experiences as well, for instance, experiences of recollection, anticipation, consummation, continuity, change, emotion, imagination, valuation, judgment, intention, and choice."[6] Asking about these experiences from the vantage point of our sacred humanity helps protect us against influential tendencies to seek the essence of true religiosity in a faith understood solely as supernatural revelation, or in a belief system that provides a normative vocabulary for its adherents. We also resist, as Du Bois did, explanations of religious valuing as merely a by-product of social and psychological processes—a by-product that has, at best, instrumental value, or is, at worse, a superstitious survival from earlier, less sophisticated times.

In this work, the religious valuing implied in conceptualizing sacred humanity should not be viewed as an objective philosophy, nor conflated with social institutions, nor reduced to subjective experiences alone. Current theories of subjectivism—including those of cultural relativism, psychologism, Freudian and Neo-Freudian psychoanalysis, behaviorism, Sartrean existentialism, and linguistic analyses—can only begin to hint at the richness of religious realities. The complex and diverse range of religious phenomena itself suggests that any reductionist approach to religiousness will itself be challenged by certain historical and empirical realities. Rather, my model of African American religious naturalism helps to disclose the hermeneutic dimension of human existence, which is not reducible to our categorizations of myriad *somethings* of life. Granted, with the idea of sacred humanity, we assume our capacity to reflect on aspects of our personality or subjectivity, which for most of us is constituted as a perceived unity of some kind; we assume that we also desire a sense of the whole; and, beyond this, that we seek to provide standards of virtue for the various tasks to which we apply ourselves as we relate to others. This latter component often involves constructing a set of judgments that brings together our knowledge of "what is" with our expectations of "what ought to be." In short, African American religious naturalism implies a type of religious valuing wherein an integrative understanding of human desires and perceptions help constitute us as relational, becoming entities. In the process, we are concerned with posing and answering the following key questions: What is true? What ought to be? How ought we to act? What may be good for us? For what may we hope? Why live at all?

An Invitation to Wonder, Mystery, and Ecological Awareness

The African American religious discourse I have featured in this book declares that blacks experience their relational humanity with a sense of wonder and awe. Ever mindful of the skepticism of Du Bois and Baldwin toward doctrinal dogmatism and otherworldly devotions, this model of religious naturalism emphasizes living life here and now as we contemplate

the mystery of being here—now, in this moment. Instead of maintaining a myopic focus on moralistic principles that superimpose life-denying strictures, this African American religious naturalism invites us to the transformative experience of wonder that comes from a profound appreciation of our embodied existence. Experiencing the sublime grandeur of nature through our senses can be awe-inspiring on at least the same level as established and accepted forms of religious art or music. Anyone who has lain under the stars at night and marveled at the vastness of the universe can attest to this feeling. A wave of different emotions can sweep over an individual, offering the sense that one is part of an amazing set of processes, and, at the same time, making one justifiably humble in acknowledging individual insignificance.

Likewise, the element of mystery also comes to the fore when pondering the unfathomable universe. Although science has managed to explain the basic structure and components of the universe, every question that it has solved has spawned countless others. In fact, the more we have explored the universe, the more we have realized that the universe inherently contains mystery. We no longer view the universe as a collection of particles existing at discreet points, but rather as moving particles spread out in a cloud of probability when not interacting with anything. Heisenberg's uncertainty principle suggests that we can never simultaneously know the exact location and exact momentum of any particle. These realizations are themselves mind-boggling. Human beings do not experience anything comparable in our day-to-day lives. In the macroscopic world, the same effect always follows its cause. No matter how many times I try to walk through the door without opening it, I will always hit the door and risk the possibility of becoming injured. However, on the subatomic scale, according to the Heisenberg uncertainty principle, theoretically there is some probability, albeit extremely small, that one of the times I walk toward the door I may pass right through it. My basic point here is that quantum mechanics demonstrates that at a fundamental level, it is not possible to measure and know everything that is going on in the universe. Observations like these are the reason some scientists and most religious naturalists are drawn to science in the first place; they evoke emotional feelings of awe and wonder that are endemic to learning about the intricacies and complexities of the natural world.

In *Reinventing the Sacred: A New View of Science, Reason, and Religion*, Stuart Kauffman argues that the evolution of the universe, biosphere, the human economy, human culture, and human action is profoundly creative. The biosphere has no direction as to how it should evolve and sustain itself, but it does so all the same. New adaptations arise spontaneously, and we can only try to explain them afterward. As he suggests, this vast tangled bank of life, the most complex system we know of in the universe, arose all on its own.[7] Kauffman argues that although physics has been able to explain the natural laws for interactions between matter and space, there exists no natural law that can explain these creative processes. This fact in itself can inspire a tremendous sense of wonder in us. Not only do we lack sufficient evidence to explain and predict future adaptations that evolve in these systems, but also, due to their inherent nature, we may never be able to do so. For Kaufmann, the notion "God" symbolizes this natural, ceaseless creativity inherent in the universe. He writes: "Is it, then, more amazing to think that an Abrahamic transcendent, omnipotent, omniscient God created everything around us, all that we participate in, in six days, or that it all arose with no transcendent Creator God, all on its own? I believe the latter is so stunning, so overwhelming, so worthy of awe, gratitude, and respect, that it is God enough for many of us. God, a fully natural God, is the very creativity in the universe."[8] Kaufman's language may be appealing to those inclined to imbue traditional religious symbolism with new meanings.

In the twenty-first century, we are developing new premises regarding nature that challenge the dominant trajectory of ideas and methods derived from such seventeenth-century figures as Bacon, Descartes, and Newton. Instead of immutable order, or change as rearrangement, we now understand nature to be evolutionary, dynamic, and emergent. We see historicity as a basic characteristic of nature, and science itself as historically conditioned. Second, in place of full determinism, we now speak of a complex combination of law and chance in fields as diverse as quantum physics, thermodynamics, and biological evolution. Both structure and openness characterize nature. Additionally, as referenced earlier, recent developments in Big Bang cosmology offer viable and sound reasoning for challenging explicit anthropocentricism. The world evolves naturally, based on the interconnection and interaction of all of its fundamental components. Such nonreductionist scientific reasoning and imagery can provide humans with a feeling of community with the entire natural world, even while maintaining the mystery and ambiguity that is central to religious experiences. Compelled by these insights, we deepen our appreciation of other-than-human nature, exploring and emphasizing our connectedness to all that is. Wendell Barry suggests that our grasp and explorations of our kinship with one another and the natural world involves a sense of propriety. As he notes, the value of this term is in "its reference to the fact that we are not alone. . . . It acknowledges the always-pressing realities of context and of influence; we cannot speak or act or live out of context. Our life inescapably affects other lives, which inescapably affect our life."[9] Barry's invitation for us to consider *propriety* in our kinship with each other is a gentle reminder of the dangers and illusion of rampant individualism. As he writes: "To raise the issue of propriety is to deny that any individual's wish is the ultimate measure of the world."[10]

Given these truths, how can we not help but have strong feelings of community, not only among ourselves as humans, but also between the entire natural world and ourselves? Notwithstanding the cultural and national differences and specificities we construct, humans are all genetically connected and part of a greater whole; as Baldwin reminds us, any harm done to another human being is essentially harm done to ourselves. Therefore, advancing this African American religious naturalism means adamantly advocating kindness, empathy, and compassion for all natural processes, not just for human others. With the capacity to influence one another and other natural processes, humans also have a responsibility to act in ways that promote the flourishing of all life, and to urge other humans who may be less aware of our interconnectedness to do the same. In short, the promises of religious naturalism are echoed in this assertion from Rue:

> Religious naturalists will then be known by their reverence and awe before Nature, their love for Nature and natural forms, their sympathy for all living things, their guilt for enlarging the ecological footprints, their pride in reducing them, their sense of gratitude directed towards the matrix of life, their contempt for those who abstract themselves from natural values, and their solidarity with those who link their self-esteem to sustainable living.[11]

Religious Valuing and Cultural Transformations

With the notion of sacred humanity, I suggest we consider forming communities of affinity, or like-mindedness, in which people of diverse ethnic and racial identities perceive what they have in common—a common creed, a historical legacy, a set of concerns and values—and are persuaded by this notion of commonality to see the humanity of one another. Such humanistic recognition must also be unperturbed by other equally important identity markers, such as socioeconomic status, sexual orientation, gender identity and expression, bodily configurations, and so forth. In suggesting this effort of community-building, however, I do not mean to imply that everyone within an expanded community of affinity do the same things, or look at the world from the same point of view. Rather, what would make such a community realistic would be human beings who understand that their shared concerns call each of them to respond to one another and to their perceived pivotal values with as much integrity and integrated knowledge as possible.

Existing within an affinity community presupposes an active commitment to sharing perceived common concerns, and to caring for one another. Ideally, this caring begins with reflexive understanding from within the actual members present. And, yet, a word of caution is needed when advancing this perspective: based on historiographical analyses, this model of human interaction has been obscured by the harsh realities of misogyny, homophobia, ethnic and cultural biases, unjust power relations, and the authoritative models of leadership that have plague many traditional religious traditions. An invaluable lesson to be gleaned from these older, established religious communities and traditions is that in spite of such sobering historical realities, ongoing and reflexive, dialogical relations with others and with the group's established value system is paramount and never exhausted. In other words, religious valuing persists, and with it the always important presuppositions regarding the nature of the human being who simultaneously does the valuing and is served by the value system itself.

These reflections lead to another important point, namely, that the concept of sacred humanity continues to inspire some of us to think and hope beyond what seems immediate and available. Given the realities of racism and other cultural forms of violence that continue to haunt all Americans in the twenty-first century, we may very well ask whether religious valuing can help us overcome some of the nihilistic tendencies and indifference that presently affect many of us. The existentialists (and most recently, the poststructuralists) are right in arguing that a metaphysical grounding of our beliefs is not necessary, or even theoretically plausible; yet for some of us, the simple ahistorical acceptance of the absurd is itself absurd and very dangerous. This does not mean, of course, revulsion from the complexities, tensions, and ambiguities that assail us daily—such qualities are to be lived and not resolved or controlled through tyrannical reason or slavish emotions. Compelled by the expansive view of humanity featured in the African American religious naturalism I describe, we may evoke a mode of valuing that simultaneously remains open to the mystery of existence and increasingly critiques those forms of social relations, cultural formations, and ideational systems that would deny others and us a basic dignified existence.

   While the religious valuing implied in this model of African American religious naturalism cannot be reduced to epistemological certitude, neither can it be divorced from cultural manifestations. This religious valuing suggests a mode of being human in the world that may be variously described as a particular pattern of discernible behaviors, a distinct set of commitments, a life-stance, or even one's basic response and openness to life in its varied historical and cultural manifestations. This lived reality is ontologically prior to any one particular expression in creed, ritual, and group interaction. At the same time, it is inseparable from these cultural expressions, and cannot be distilled out and objectified. Although we can no longer presume that grasping the meaning of the totality of human experience or of cultural life is possible, as sacred humans we can continue to construct appropriate symbols, in language and in action, to express our reflective comprehensions and emotional commitments to certain forms of cultural life. This type of religious valuing, then, becomes one dimension of cultural transformation that evolves as our thinking evolves. More importantly, with this orientation we are led away from a modernist view that demands an "all or nothing" epistemological framework and toward one that takes into account our complex historicity and our radical relatedness as sacred humans, and all the possible nuances associated with that phrase.

   Additionally, if African American religious naturalism is to assume a meaningful place in contemporary U.S. culture, it must provide sympathetic understandings of (and critical responses to) the diverse worlds we live in, without necessarily clashing with other forms of human knowledge or withdrawing into a self-serving universalism. This type of religious valuing must be versatile enough to adapt to ever-changing cultural situations; yet it must also be conceptually sophisticated and symbolically rich in content, so that we are able to absorb more positively the dizziness resulting from the complexity and multiplicities of human life in all its myriad splendor and pain. As indicated above, it is increasingly unsatisfactory to view any form of religious valuing as a separable module of human experience, because the need for meaningful commitment intrudes into virtually every contemporary reflection.

   Recalling Du Bois's invitation to his contemporaries to join others as "co-workers in the kingdom of culture," I invite a new generation of cultural workers inspired by the vision of sacred humanity to "self-consciously situate themselves at vulnerable conjunctional modes of ongoing disciplinary discourses where each of them posits nothing less than new objects of knowledge, new praxes of humanist (in the broad sense of the word) activity, new theoretical models that upset or at the least radically alter the prevailing paradigmatic norms."[12] Inspired by the work begun by our ancients, contemporary African Americans inspired by this vision of sacred humanity must continue to conduct our thinking and investigating through various forms of resistance and struggle. Accordingly, we are led to ask: Which cultural values are esteemed, and under which conditions? Which institutional props or mechanisms aid in reproducing or contesting influential cultural artifacts? To what extent, and how, do our institutionalized values aid in the myriad struggles to acquire, maintain, or resist expansive views of our humanity?

Advancing this type of religiosity as critical cultural work, we can expect (and should hope) to encounter capacious views of our shared humanity in the fullness of their material and conceptual forms. And we should not be unaware of the power dimension of our value-laden discourses, for such awareness leads us toward strategic practices that may help to advance some of our interests. If empirical, historicist analysis has taught us anything, it is that thinking, reflective subjects are also material and partisan, situated in cultural formations that are themselves contested sites of power/knowledge struggle between different social groups and classes, which can change in one particular direction or another. Wherever there are different interests in play, individuals and social groups will develop strategies to realize or protect those interests with which they identify. In this moment, then, there is the crucial notion that our convictions and our systems of thought are contingent, strategic, in constant flux, and marked by undecidability.

With this form of religious naturalism and its sacred humanity concept, we are embodying a novel type of spatiality in the current landscape where alternative values, social practices, and theorizations are necessarily intermingled. While recognizing that we will be challenged to identify and promote a set of assumptions, positions, critiques, and so forth that are grounded in political and ethical commitments, we are nonetheless inspired by this persuasive model of humanity as interdependent relationality. The fuller work of creating alternative cultural values and ethical mandates will include localized counterhegemonic practices of relationality. In more practical terms, we must recognize that the institutions and procedures that we employ to actualize hierarchies of value—religious institutions and traditions, schools, universities, prisons, local and national government, political organizations of all kinds—are always likely to become fixated by the desire to conserve and reproduce those value structures. Yet in keeping with the constructive tasks of religious naturalism, we remind religious practitioners to institute practices that allow for pluralization.

For instance, as we determine to honor the view of human beings as centers of value, or as human destinies, we should be prepared to encounter myriad formulations of gender, racial, class, and erotic constructions. In other words, we see that forms of valuing must themselves be pluralized.

While addressing critical literacy, Colin McFaren and Peter Lankshear have suggested that in order to reclaim their right to live humanly, marginalized groups must not only theorize and analyze but also confront, in praxis, those institutions, processes, and ideologies that prevent them from, as Paulo Freire puts it, "naming their world."[13] The model of African American religious naturalism I endorse in this study can be viewed as one avenue toward this end. It inspires us to be often strategic, even politically savvy, in our efforts to implement instances of alternative valuing, which may lead to new and expanded forms of sacred humanity. With the concept of sacred humanity, this discourse also considers new ways of engaging our religious sensibilities to enhance our complex humanity, helping us engage the many worlds of kinship that constitute our being here. As I noted above when discussing the merits of the discourses of Cooper, Bu Bois and Baldwin, as long as certain configurations of the world exist—what some of us would call asymmetrical social and power relations—there will be the need for alternative cultural values and ethical mandates.

The recognition that theories do not yield "Truth" but constitute different, competing versions of reality that are tied to specific social interests is central to cultural critique. Thus, with the concept of sacred humanity, we can dream of different practices, of expanded configurations of relationality, of new worlds—holding up a historicizing mirror to current society that compels a recognition of its transitory and fallible nature, such that more people realize that "what is" can be disassembled and improved.

In looking forward to and enacting this critical consciousness, we are inspired by the spirit of Du Bois, as poignantly symbolized in the following reflection: "Had it not been for the race problem early thrust upon me and enveloping me, I should have probably been an unquestioning worshipper at the shrine of the established order into which I was born. But just that part of this order which seemed to most of my fellows nearest perfection seemed to me most inequitable and wrong; and starting from that critique, I gradually, as the years went by, found other things to question in my environment."[14] With our emphasis on the necessity of conceiving humans as centers of values, this naturalistic model of African American religiosity continues to inspire cultural critics, poets, artists, and political leaders to conceive of new worlds, and to hope beyond what seems immediate and available by investing in our *sacred* humanity.

Acknowledgments

Various persons and organizations have lent support and contributed to the publication of this work. I first thank Thomas Lay, Acquisitions Editor of Fordham University Press, for his initial interest in this study, and for that pivotal conversation at Drew University in 2014 that serendipitously led to the publication of *Black Lives and Sacred Humanity* by Fordham University Press.

I am immensely grateful to Richard Morrison, Editorial Director at Fordham University Press, who enthusiastically embraced this study upon introduction. I have enjoyed working with Richard and the editorial staff at the Press, deeply appreciative of the care with which they reviewed the original manuscript and helped prepare it for publication. I am indebted to Eric Newman and his staff for the meticulous copy editing and offer a special word of thanks to Eric for his help in addressing some software glitches. I also thank the anonymous reviewers of the manuscript for their insightful comments and varied suggestions, which helped transform it into a more compelling, thoughtful book.

I also acknowledge, with profound thanks, the encouragement and support of various colleagues who heard me present aspects of this study in the last few years: Lea Schweitz, Mike Hogue, and the students and staff at the Zygon Center for the Study of Religion; the international group of scholars attending Oxford University's Religious Studies Symposium; the cohort of students and scholars in attendance at Drew's Thirteenth Transdisciplinary Theological Colloquium on Science, Religion, and Materiality who enthusiastically welcomed my religious naturalist perspective; Whitney Bauman, whose steadfast support and kind invitation led to my presenting a portion of this work at the 2015 Institute on Religion in an Age of Science conference on Star Island, New Hampshire; and my colleagues in the Religious Studies Department at Bucknell University who read aspects of the work and engaged me in lively conversation during formal gatherings at which we shared our scholarship.

Heartfelt thanks are due to Catherine Keller of Drew Theological School, whose ideas, friendship, and support of my scholarship through the years have sustained and inspired me. I am exceedingly grateful to Maria Antonaccio for her graceful presence in my life, and for being a wonderful friend with whom I have experienced many stimulating, enlightening conversations. I also acknowledge, with thanks, the genuine support of friends Marion Brown and Lisa Strayer, with whom I share an uncompromising love of nature.

Genuine thanks are also extended to my siblings (Melvin, Billy, Vanessa, George, Jacquelyn, Brian, Sean, and Latria) for their unceasing love and devotion. I also offer a special word of thanks to Lane Eib, whose loving and supportive friendship during the formative writing period of this project was a gift to me. Finally, I offer profound thanks to Jannie Mae White, my exquisite mother. Her continual and unceasing support of my professional life and passion for writing keeps me sustained and smiling. I dedicate this book to her and to Luther White, Jr., whose immeasurable love for their children reverberates throughout these pages.

INTRODUCTION: IN SEARCH OF A NEW RELIGIOUS IDEAL

1. W. E. B. Du Bois, "Of the Faith of the Fathers," in *The Souls of Black Folk*, ed. Henry Louis Gates, Jr. and Terri Hume Oliver, A Norton & Company Critical Edition (New York: W. W. Norton, 1999), 129.

2. Du Bois's attentiveness to the passivity required by Christianity and its concomitant otherworldly focus among many Africans Americans was matched by his focus on the ethical intent of freed blacks whose religious fervor was directed toward their full freedom. These appraisals led him to identify two conflicting, agonistic religious impulses among African Americans during his time, symbolized by the cultural activities and values of the South and the North. Du Bois consequently juxtaposes the deceptive lives of the southern blacks, who dare not speak "real thoughts, real aspirations," with those of the radical, excessively critical northern blacks, whose "souls are bitter at the fate which drops the Veil between." Notwithstanding these critical judgments of black culture and its inherent ethical (or religious) paradoxes, Du Bois never fails to underscore the functional value of black religion as the highest aspiration of the African American character: its claim on life, so to speak.

3. Loyal Rue, "Redefining Myth and Religion: Introduction to a Conversation," in *Zygon: Journal of Religion and Science* 29 (September 1994): 316. Following Rue's lead in both rejecting any form of supernaturalism and resisting the ever-increasing, popular forms of reductionist naturalism, I view my work as a variant of contemporary religious naturalism.

4. Here I am alluding to current trends in cognitive science approaches to God-belief, which I discuss briefly in chapter 2.

5. Charles Long, *Significations: Signs, Symbols, and Images in the Interpretation of Religion* (Aurora, Co.: Davies Group Publishers, 1999).

6. Cornel West, *Prophesy Deliverance! An Afro-American Revolutionary Christianity* (Louisville: Westminster John Knox Press, 2002); Victor Anderson, *Beyond Ontological Blackness: An Essay on African American Religious and Cultural Criticism* (New York: Continuum International Publishing Group, 1999); Anthony Pinn, *Varieties of African American Religious Experience* (Min-

neapolis: Augsburg Fortress Press, 1998) and *By These Hands: A Documentary History of African American Humanism* (New York: NYU Press, 2001).

7. Anthony Pinn, *Terror and Triumph* (Minneapolis: Augsburg Fortress Press, 2003) and *What Is African American Religion?* (Minneapolis: Augsburg Fortress Press, 2011).

8. Russell T. McCutcheon, *The Discipline of Religion: Structure, Meaning, Rhetoric* (New York: Routledge, 2003).

1. AFRICAN AMERICAN RELIGIOUS SENSIBILITIES AND THE QUESTION OF THE HUMAN

1. In this study, I use *African American* and *black* as interchangeable terms for the same cultural phenomenon and received tradition that provides a sense of group identity for contemporary U.S. citizens of African descent who trace their lineage to the historical matrix of slavery and its aftermath in successive centuries. Also, while acknowledging the diverse forms of black religious expression that have emerged in the last several hundred years, I focus on the dominant vein of Christianity and its supernaturalism when identifying a trajectory of African American religious expression.

2. Cornel West and Eddie S. Glaude, Jr., "Towards New Visions and New Approaches," in *African American Religious Thought*, ed. Cornel West and Eddie S. Glaude, Jr. (Louisville: Westminster John Knox Press, 2003), xiii–xv.

3. See A. Leon Higginbotham, Jr., and Barbara Kopytoff, "Property First, Humanity Second: The Recognition of the Slave's Human Nature in Virginia Civil Law," *Ohio State Law Journal* 50 (Summer 1989): 511–40; William M. Wiecek, "The Statutory Law of Slavery and Race in the Thirteen Mainland Colonies of British America," *The William and Mary Quarterly*, 34, no. 2 (April 1977): 258–80; A. Leon Higginbotham, Jr., *In the Matter of Color: Race and the American Legal Process: The Colonial Period* (New York: Oxford University Press, 1980).

4. William W. Fisher III, "Ideology and Imagery in the Law of Slavery: Symposium on the Law," *Chicago-Kent Law Review* 68, no. 3 (1992), art. 4, 1051–83. See also Andrew Fede, *People Without Rights: An Interpretation of the Fundamentals of the Law of Slavery in the U.S. South* (New York: Routledge: 2012), 34ff.

5. Since its inception, Critical Race Theory (CRT) has been intent on examining existing power structures, seeking to show that racism is engrained in the fabric and system of American society. CRT asserts that institutional racism is omnipresent in the dominant culture and not dependent on the existence of individual racists. Within legal scholarship, CRT has rejected the traditions of liberalism and meritocracy, which help uphold the assumption

that the law is neutral and colorblind. CRT has also challenged the cultural narratives that purport to advance a view of meritocracy (e.g., that everyone who works hard can attain wealth, power, and privilege), which ignores the systemic inequalities that institutional racism creates. For further articulations of CRT in legal scholarship and other fields, see Kimberlé Crenshaw and Neil Gotando, eds., *Critical Race Theory: The Key Writings that Formed the Movement* (New York: New Press, 1996); Richard Delgado and Jean Stefancic, eds., *Critical Race Theory: An Introduction* (New York: NYU Press, 2012); Jean Stefancic and Richard Delgado, eds., *Critical Race Theory: The Cutting Edge*, 3rd ed. (Philadelphia: Temple University Press, 2013); P. S. Rothenberg, ed., *White Privilege: Essential Readings on the Other Side of Racism* (New York: Macmillan, 2007); Linda M. Alcoff, "What Should White People Do?" *Hypatia* 13, no. 3 (1998): 6–26; Shannon Sullivan and Nancy Tuana, eds., *Race and Epistemologies of Ignorance*, Philosophy and Race series (Albany: SUNY Press, 2007).

6. James H. Evans, Jr., *We Have Been Believers: An African-American Systematic Theology* (Minneapolis: Augsburg Fortress Press, 1992), 100. See also Winthrop D. Jordan, *The White Man's Burden: Historical Origins of Racism in the United States* (New York: Oxford University Press, 1974), 3–25.

7. Albert J. Roboteau, *A Fire in the Bones: Reflections on African-American Religious History* (Boston: Beacon Press, 1995) and *Slave Religion: The "Invisible Institution" in the Antebellum South* (New York: Oxford University Press, 1980); Dwight Hopkins and George Cummings, eds., *Cut Loose Your Stammering Tongue: Black Theology in the Slave Narratives* (Maryknoll, N.Y.: Orbis, 1991; 2nd ed., Louisville, Ky.: Westminster John Knox Press, 2003); Earl R. Riggins, *Dark Symbols, Obscure Signs: God, Self, and Community in the Slave Mind* (Maryknoll, N.Y.: Orbis), 1993.

8. John Salillant, "Origins of African American Biblical Hermeneutics in Eighteenth-Century Black Opposition to the Slave Trade and Slavery," in *African Americans and the Bible: Sacred Texts and Social Textures*, ed. Vincent L. Wimbush (New York: Continuum, 2003), 236–37; Roboteau, *Fire in the Bones*, 28. See also E. Franklin Frazier, *The Negro Church in America* (New York: Schocken Books, 1974), 24; 60–68; Eddie S. Glaude, Jr., *Exodus! Religion, Race, and Nation in Early Nineteenth-Century Black America* (Chicago: University of Chicago Press, 2000), 4ff.

9. Sojourner Truth, *Narrative of Sojourner Truth* (New York: Penguin Classics, 1998); Alexander Crummell, *Destiny and Race: Selected Writings, 1840–1898*, ed. William Jeremy Moses (Amherst: University of Massachusetts Press, 1992).

10. Maria Stewart, *Productions of Mrs. Maria W. Stewart* (Boston: Friends of Freedom and Virtue, 1835), reprinted in Sue E. Houchins, ed., *Spiritual*

Narratives, Schomburg Library of Nineteenth-Century Black Women Writers series (New York: Oxford University Press, 1988), 59.

11. Maria Stewart, "Duty of Females," *The Liberator* (May 5, 1832), cited in *Early Negro Writing, 1760–1837*, ed. Dorothy Parker (Boston: Beacon Press, 1971), 124.

12. Stewart, *Productions of Mrs. Maria W. Stewart*, 75, 76.

13. Scholars of African American religious thought and history continue to debate the effects of Christianity on African slaves, whether it should be viewed as a coercive force used by slave owners to control them, or looked upon as a means of helping slaves survive the harrowing conditions of slavery. Some slaves certainly became Christians voluntarily, because it helped them endure hardships and gave them reason for hope, or because membership offered other benefits. According to some accounts, many slave owners felt that Christian slaves would be more obedient (although this didn't turn out to be true) and therefore encouraged conversion. However, many owners later came to feel that Christianity may actually have encouraged rebellion, and began to discourage Christian missionaries from preaching to the slaves. For further reading, see Major J. Jones, *The Color of God: The Concept of God in Afro-American Thought* (Macon, Ga: Mercer University Press, 1987), and Kurt Buhring, *Conceptions of God, Freedom, and Ethics in African American and Jewish Theology*, Black Religion / Womanist Thought / Social Justice series (New York: Palgrave Macmillan, 2008).

14. E. Franklin Frazier, *The Negro Church in America* (New York: Schocken Books, 1974), 24; 60–68.

15. See Benjamin E. Mays, *The Negro's God, as Reflected in His Literature* (Boston: Chapman and Grimes, 1938; reprint, Eugene, Ore.: Wipf and Stock, 2010).

16. Clifton H. Johnson, ed., *God Struck Me Dead: Voices of Ex-Slaves* (Philadelphia: United Church Press, 1969), 14.

17. Evans, *We Have Been Believers*, 54.

18. Ibid., 67.

19. Cone's early work represents the classic expression of black liberation theology. See James Cone, *A Black Theology of Liberation*, C. Eric Lincoln Series in Black Religion (Philadelphia and New York: J. B. Lippincott Company, 1970), and *Black Theology and Black Power* (New York: Harper and Row, 1969). For contemporary accounts of African American and other liberation theologies, see Anthony Pinn and Stacy Floyd-Thomas, eds., *Liberation Theologies in the United States: An Introduction* (New York: NYU Press, 2010); Dwight Hopkins, *Introducing Black Theology of Liberation* (Maryknoll, N.Y.: Orbis Books, 1999) and *Black Faith and Public Talk: Essays in Honor of James Cone's Black Theology and Black Power* (Maryknoll, N.Y.: Orbis, 1999).

20. For representational texts, see Cornel West, *Prophesy Deliverance! An Afro-American Revolutionary Christianity* (Louisville: Westminster John Knox Press, 2002); Victor Anderson, *Beyond Ontological Blackness: An Essay on African American Religious and Cultural Criticism* (New York: Continuum International Publishing Group, 1999); Anthony Pinn, *Varieties of African American Religious Experience* (Minneapolis: Ausburg Fortress Press, 1998); James D. Evans, *Black Theology: A Critical Assessment and Annotated Bibliography* (San Francisco: Greenwood Press, April 1987) and *We Have Been Believers*; Dwight Hopkins, *Being Human: Race, Culture, and Religion* (Minneapolis: Fortress Press, 2005) and *Heart and Head: Black Theology—Past, Present, and Future* (New York: Palgrave, 2002); Theodore Walker, *Mothership Connections: A Black Atlantic Synthesis of Neoclassical Metaphysics and Black Theology* (Albany: SUNY Press, 2004); Jacquelyn Grant, *White Women's Christ and Black Women's Jesus: Feminist Christology and Womanist Response* (Atlanta: Scholars Press, 1989); Emilie Townes, *A Troubling in My Soul: Womanist Perspectives on Evil and Suffering* (Maryknoll, N.Y.: Orbis, 1993) and *Womanist Justice, Womanist Hope* (New York: Oxford University Press, 2000); Monica A. Coleman, *Making a Way Out of No Way: A Womanist Theology* (Minneapolis: Fortress Press, 2008).

21. One of the earliest articulations of womanist religious thought was offered in 1987 by Delores Williams in "Womanist Theology: Black Women's Voices," *Christianity and Crisis*, March 2, 1987; http://www.religion-online .org/showarticle.asp?title=445. For further reading of representative texts, see Katie Geneva Cannon, *Black Womanist Ethics* (Atlanta: Scholars Press, 1988); Delores Williams, "Womanist Theology," in *Weaving the Visions: New Patterns in Feminist Spirituality*, ed. Judith Plaskow and Carol P. Christ (San Francisco: Harper and Row, 1989); Jacquelyn Grant, ed., *Perspectives on Womanist Theology* (Atlanta: ITC Press, 1995); Linda Thomas, *Living Stones in the Household of God: The Legacy and Future of Black Theology* (Minneapolis: Fortress Press, 2004); Emilie Townes, *Embracing the Spirit: Womanist Perspectives on Hope, Salvation, and Transformation* (Maryknoll, N.Y.: Orbis, 1997) and *Womanist Ethics and the Cultural Production of Evil* (New York: Palgrave Macmillan, 2006); Traci West, *Disruptive Christian Ethics: When Racism and Women's Lives Matter* (Louisville: Westminster John Knox Press, 2006); Monica Coleman, *Making a Way Out of No Way: A Womanist Theology* (Minneapolis: Fortress Press, 2008); Karen Baker-Fletcher, *Sisters of Dust, Sisters of Spirit: Womanist Wordings on God and Creation* (Minneapolis: Fortress Press, 1998) and "A Womanist Journey," in *Deeper Shades of Purple: Womanism in Religion and Society*, ed. Stacy M. Floyd-Thomas (New York: New York University Press, 2006), 158–75.

22. Loyal Rue, *Religion Is Not about God: How Spiritual Traditions Nurture Our Biological Nature and What To Do When They Fail* (New Brunswick, N.J.:

Rutgers University Press, 2005), 1. In his naturalist approach, Rue describes different religious traditions as a series of strategies that aim to influence human nature so that we might think, feel, and act in ways that are good for us, both individually and collectively. Employing images, symbols, and rituals, religion's main goals are to promote reproductive fitness and survival through the facilitation of harmonious social relations.

23. Ibid., 3. Rue continues: "Kant identified religion with achieving rational coherence in human experience; Feuerbach believed religion was a covert way of coming to terms with self-alienation; Marx analyzed religion in terms of its ability to cope with the dehumanizing consequences of economic exploitation; Durkheim associated religion with a veneration of the social order; and Freud described religion as the projection of deep psychological dynamics."

24. See West, *Prophesy Deliverance!*; Anderson, *Beyond Ontological Blackness*; and Anthony Pinn, *A Documentary History of African American Humanism* (New York: NYU Press, 2001) and *Varieties of African American Religious Experience*.

25. Vincent Lloyd, "Black Secularism and Black Theology," *Theology Today* 68, no. 1 (2011): 1–5. See also Thabiti M. Anyabwile, *The Decline of African American Theology* (Downers Grove, Ill.: IVP Academic, 2007).

26. Charles Taylor, *A Secular Age* (Cambridge, Mass.: Belknap Press of Harvard University Press, 2007), 19ff.

27. Stephen Mitchell, *Gilgamesh: A New English Version* (New York: Free Press: 2004).

28. As a philosophical, classical African concept, the word *ubuntu* has its origins in several of the Bantu languages of Southern Africa. It is at its core an ethical or humanist ideology, referring to the necessity of unity and the removal of self-serving practices in order for the human race to evolve, to exist peacefully, and especially to prosper. A cornerstone of the "New South Africa" (post-apartheid), the concept of *ubuntu* has been used since the first democratic elections in 1994 (as a founding principle, in fact) in order to demonstrate the way the country should operate and be run politically. The human ethics and moral scope that *ubuntu* implies is seen to be an admirable compass for political decision-making. For further readings on the complex history, evolution, and usage of this term, see Sakiemi Idoniboye-Obu and Ayo Whetho, "Ubuntu: 'You are because I am' or 'I am because you are'?" in *Alternation* 20, no. 1(2013): 229–47; Christian B. N. Gade, "What is Ubuntu? Different Interpretations among South Africans of African Descent," *South African Journal of Philosophy* 31, no. 3(2012): 484–503; Hanneke Stuit, "Ubuntu, the Truth and Reconciliation Commission, and South African National Identity," *Thamyris / Intersecting* 20 (2010): 83–102; L. Praeg,

"An Answer to the Question: 'What Is Ubuntu?'" *South African Journal of Philosophy* 27, no. 4 (2008): 367–85; C. I. Tshoose, "The Emerging Role of the Constitutional Value of Ubuntu for Informal Social Security in South Africa," *African Journal of Legal Studies* 3, no. 1 (2009): 12–19; T. Metz, "Ubuntu as a Moral Theory: Reply to Four Critics," *South African Journal of Philosophy* 26, no. 4 (2007): 369–87; Desmond Tutu, *No Future without Forgiveness* (London: Rider, 1999).

29. In its broadest sense, *value theory* is a catch-all label in philosophical thinking that encompasses an evaluative aspect. In values discourse, types of values include ethical/moral values, doctrinal/ideological (religious/political) values, social values, and aesthetic values. Furthermore, the history of value theory includes debates on whether some values are innate. In some systems where there is a hierarchy of values, subordinate values derive all of their value from a relation to a supreme value, single value, or highest good that justifies the rest. One exemplary model is Platonism, which posits the form of the Good as beyond being, or transcendent. Accordingly, the Good is the source of the reality of other forms and also of their copies in the visible realm. Later medieval philosophers appropriated this hierarchy of values, establishing in various metaphysical systems the concept of God as the Highest Good, or, in more familiar terms, as the most perfect being and the source of all other beings. For a sampling of works in values discourse, including ethical works, see Aristotle, *Nicomachean Ethics*, in *The Complete Works of Aristotle: The Revised Oxford Translation*, ed. J. Barnes (Princeton: Princeton University Press, 1984); Immanuel Kant, *Groundwork for the Metaphysics of Morals* [1785], trans. Mary Gregor (Cambridge: Cambridge University Press, 1997); Richard Kraut, *What Is Good and Why: The Ethics of Well-Being* (Cambridge: Harvard University Press, 2007); Joseph Raz, *Engaging Reason: On the Theory of Value and Action* (Oxford: Oxford University Press, 1999); Susan Wolf, *The Variety of Values: Essays on Morality, Meaning, and Love* (Oxford: Oxford University Press, 2014) and *Meaning in Life and Why It Matters* (Princeton: Princeton University Press, 2012); Michael Zimmerman, *The Nature of Intrinsic Value* (Lanham, Md.: Rowman and Littlefield, 2001).

30. Mark C. Taylor, *Erring: A Postmodern A/Theology* (Chicago: University of Chicago Press, 1986), 4.

31. Ibid., 22.

32. Trends within twentieth-century liberal theology have ranged from the historic-critical research of Ritschl, through the social gospel movement of Rauschenbusch, the Neo-orthodoxy of Barth, Brunner and Bultmann, and Reinhold Neibuhr, to the empirical/process orientations of the Chicago School of the 1930s and 1940s. In the latter part of the twentieth century, such post–World War II liberal movements as the existentialism

of Macquarrie and Tillich represented the modern search for new foundations. This list is not fully representative of the complexity and diversity of
liberal theology. It does, however, list some of the major post-Enlightenment
Protestant scholars who were concerned with the vitality and necessity of
religious interpretations in an increasingly secularized society. For representative works, see Paul Tillich, *Systematic Theology*, vol. 1 (Chicago: University of Chicago Press, 1967) and *Dynamics of Faith* (New York: Harper
and Brothers, 1958); Emil Brunner, *Man in Revolt* (Louisville: Westminster
John Knox Press, 1979); Reinhold Niebuhr, *Moral Man and Immoral Society*
(Louisville: Westminster John Knox Press, 2013); John Macquarrie, *In Search
of Humanity: A Theological and Philosophical Approach* (New York: Crossroad,
1983).

33. One contemporary example is process theology, derived from the
speculative metaphysics of British thinker Alfred N. Whitehead. For further
reading, see Alfred N. Whitehead, *Process and Reality*, Harper Torchbook ed.
(New York: Harper and Row, 1960) and *Adventures of Ideas*, Mentor Books ed.
(New York: Mentor, 1933); Charles Hartshorne, *Man's Vision of God and the
Logic of Theism* (Hamden, Conn.: Archon, 1964) and *Omnipotence and Other
Theological Mistakes* (Albany: SUNY Press, 1984); Catherine Keller, *On the
Mystery: Discerning Divinity in Process* (New York: Fortress Press, 2008); Ro-
land Faber, *God as Poet of the World* (Louisville: Westminster John Knox Press,
2008); Phillip Clayton, *Adventures in the Spirit: God, World, Divine Action*
(New York: Fortress Press, 2008); David R. Griffin, *Reenchantment without
Supernaturalism* (Ithaca, N.Y.: Cornell University Press, 2001); John Cobb
and David Ray Griffin, *Process Theology: An Introductory Exposition* (Philadelphia: Westminster Press, 1976).

34. For further discussion, see Claudia Schippert, "Implications of Queer
Theory for the Study of Religion and Gender: Entering the Third Decade,"
Religion and Gender 1, no. 1 (2011), 66–84. See also Gordon Kaufmann,
"Critical Theology as a University Discipline," in *Theology and the University*, ed. David Ray Griffith and Joseph C. Hough, Jr. (Albany: SUNY Press,
1991), 35–50. This earlier articulation by Gordon Kaufman expressed the
necessity of acknowledging pluralism and dialogue in critical theology.

35. Martin Heidegger, *Identity and Difference*, trans. J. Stambaugh (New
York: Harper and Row, 1969), 55–74.

36. Taylor, *Erring*, 30.

37. Emmanuel Eze, ed., *Race and the Enlightenment* (Malden, Mass.: Blackwell Publishers, 1996), 5ff. See also David Theo Goldberg, *Racist Culture*
(Cambridge, Mass.: Blackwell Publishers, 1993).

38. For more information on the notion of certain "subjugated knowl-
edges" becoming lost amid the triumphant march of European reasoning and

progress, see Michel Foucault, *Power / Knowledge: Selected Interviews and Other Writings, 1972–77* (New York: Pantheon Books, 1980), 81–82.

39. Jean Paul Sartre, "Preface," in Frantz Fanon, *Wretched of the Earth*, trans. Constance Farrington (New York: Grove Press, 1968), 22. Insights emerging from such developments as cultural studies, feminism, and post-colonial thought show that discussions of the (liberal) political philosophies of major European voices (Jefferson, Hume, or Locke, for example) must also take into account the extent to which their doctrines were implicated in acts of racial supremacy, sexism, exploitation of other nationalities, colonialism, and slavery. For further reading, see Sandra Harding, ed., *The "Racial" Economy of Science* (Bloomington: Indiana University Press, 1993); William Tucker, *The Science and Politics of Racial Research* (Chicago: University of Illinois Press, 1994); Elazar Parkan, *The Retreat of Scientific Racism: Changing Concepts of Race in Britain and the United States between the World Wars* (Cambridge: Cambridge University Press, 1992); William B. Cohen, *The French Encounter with Africans: White Response to Blacks, 1530–1880* (Bloomington: Indiana University Press, 1980); Katherine Faull, *Anthropology and the German Enlightenment* (Lewisburg, Pa.: Bucknell and Associated University Presses, 1994); Henry Louis Gates, Jr., *"Race," Writing, and Difference* (Chicago: University of Chicago Press, 1985); George Fredrickson, *The Black Image in the White Mind: The Debate on Afro-America Character and Destiny, 1817–1914* (Hanover, Conn.: Weslyan University Press, 1987); Stephen J. Gould, *The Mismeasure of Man* (New York: W. W. Norton, 1981); Nancy Stepan, *The Idea of Race in Science: Great Britain, 1800–1960* (London: Macmillan, 1982); Leon Poliakov, *The Aryan Myth: A History of Racist and Nationalist Ideas in Europe* (New York: Basic Books, 1974).

40. For further readings, see Kwame Anthony Appiah, "Racisms," in *Anatomy of Racism*, ed. David Theo Goldberg (Minneapolis: University of Minnesota, 1990), 3–17. For recent studies, see John A. Powell, *Racing to Justice: Transforming Our Conceptions of Self and Other to Build an Inclusive Society* (Bloomington: Indiana University Press, 2012), and Jacqueline Battalora, *Birth of a White Nation: The Invention of White People and Its Relevance Today* (Houston: Strategic Book Publishing, 2013).

41. See, for example, Taylor, *Erring*; Catherine Keller and Anne Daniell, eds., *Process and Difference* (Albany, N.Y.: SUNY Press, 2002); John D. Caputo and Michael J. Scanlon, eds., *God, the Gift, and Postmodernism* (Bloomington: Indiana University Press, 1999), and John D. Caputo and Michael J. Scanlon, eds., *Transcendence and Beyond: A Postmodern Inquiry* (Bloomington: Indiana University Press, 2007); Thomas J. J. Altizer, *Deconstruction and Theology* (New York: Crossroads, 1982); Carl A. Raschke, *The Alchemy of the Word: Language and the End of Theology* (Missoula, Mont.: Scholars Press, 1979);

Jeffrey Stout, *The Flight from Authority: Religion, Morality, and the Quest for Autonomy* (Notre Dame, Ind.: University of Notre Dame Press, 1981); Charles Winquist, *Epiphanies of Darkness* (Albany: SUNY Press, 1987); Edith Wyschogrod, Carl Raschke, and David Crownfield, eds., *Lacan and Religious Discourse* (Albany: SUNY Press, 1989); David R. Griffin, *God and Religion in the Postmodern World* (Albany: SUNY Press: 1989); Kevin Hart, *The Trespass of the Sign* (Cambridge: Cambridge University Press, 1989); Graham Ward, *The Postmodern God: A Theological Reader* (Malden, Mass.: Blackwell Publishers, 1997); Terrence W. Tilley, ed., *Postmodern Theologies* (Maryknoll, N.Y.: Orbis 1995).

42. See my fuller discussion in "Religious Scriptors of Human Possibilities and Cultural Transformations," in "The Religious and the Secular," ed. Lori Branch and Everett Hamner, special issue, *Iowa Journal of Cultural Studies* 7, no. 1 (Fall 2005): 46–62.

43. Roland Barthes, "*The Death of the Author*," *Image-Music-Text* (New York: Hill and Wang, 1977), 146.

44. Ibid.

2. SACRED HUMANITY AS STUBBORN, IRREDUCIBLE MATERIALITY

1. Susan Haack, *Defending Science—Within Reason: Between Scientism and Cynicism* (Amherst, N.Y.: Prometheus Books, 2007), 344.

2. Matthew Alper, *The "God" Part of the Brain: A Scientific Interpretation of Human Spirituality and God* (Naperville, Ill.: Sourcebooks, 2006), 92–97, 207–24.

3. Richard Dawkins, *The God Delusion* (Boston: Houghton Mifflin Harcourt, 2006), 203–05; 216–22.

4. Todd Tremlin, *Minds and Gods: The Cognitive Foundations of Religion* (Oxford: Oxford University Press, 2006), 9.

5. Pascal Boyer, *Religion Explained: The Evolutionary Origins of Religious Thought* (New York: Basic Books, 2001), 298.

6. Karl Marx, *Critique of Hegel's "Philosophy of Right,"* ed. and trans. Joseph O'Malley, trans. Annette Jolin, Cambridge Studies in the History and Theory of Politics (Cambridge: Cambridge University Press, 1970); Sigmund Freud, *The Future of an Illusion* (Standard Edition), ed. James Strachey (New York: W. W. Norton, 1989).

7. See Jerome Stone, *Religious Naturalism Today: The Rebirth of a Forgotten Alternative* (Albany: SUNY Press, 2008), 1–15.

8. See, for example, Ursula Goodenough, *The Sacred Depths of Nature* (New York: Oxford University Press, 1998); Loyal Rue, *Religion is Not about God: How Spiritual Traditions Nurture Our Biological Nature and What To Do When They Fail* (New Brunswick, N.J.: Rutgers University Press, 2005); Don-

ald Crosby, *Living with Ambiguity: Religious Naturalism and the Menace of Evil* (Albany: SUNY Press, 2009).

9. Ursula Goodenough and Deacon Terrence, "From Biology to Consciousness to Morality," *Zygon Journal of Religion and Science*, 38 (4): 801–19.

10. Rue, *Religion is Not about God*, 25.

11. Stephen J. Gould, *Wonderful Life: The Burgess Shale and the Nature of History* (London: Hutchinson Radious, 1989); Terence Deacon, "The Hierarchic Logic of Emergence: Untangling the Interdependence of Evolution and Self-Organization," in *Evolution and Learning: The Baldwin Effect Reconsidered*, ed. B. Weber and D. Depen (Cambridge, Mass.: MIT Press, 2003), 273–308, and "Emergence: The Hole at the Wheel's Hub," in *Re-Emergence of Emergence*, ed. Philip Clayton and Paul Davies (Oxford: Oxford University Press, 2006).

12. Goodenough, *Sacred Depths*, 63.

13. Ibid., 40.

14. Ibid., 42, 44.

15. Ibid., 66.

16. Ibid., 71.

17. Ibid., 64.

18. Mircea Eliade, *The Sacred and the Profane* (Orlando, Fla.: Harcourt, 1987).

19. Goodenough, *Sacred Depths*, 73.

20. The development of various theories of evolution from Lamarck to Darwin was crucial to the creation of racism in the nineteenth century. For further reading, see Peter Reill, "Anti-Mechanism, Vitalism, and Their Political Implications in Late Enlightened Scientific Thought," *Francia* 16 (1989): 195–212.

21. Rue, *Religion is Not about God*, 75.

22. Carol Albright and James Ashbrooke, *The Humanizing Brain: Where Religion and Neuroscience Meet* (Cleveland: Pilgrim Press, 1997), 34; see also my brief discussion in Carol Wayne White, *The Legacy of Anne Conway (1631–1679): Reverberations of a Mystical Naturalism* (Albany: SUNY Press, 2009), 113ff.

23. Terrence W. Deacon, *The Symbolic Species: The Co-Evolution of Language and the Brain* (New York: W. W. Norton, 1997).

24. Ibid., 36ff; 45–46.

25. Michael Arbib, *The Metaphorical Brain 2: Neural Networks and Beyond* (New York: John Wiley, 1989); Joseph LeDoux, *The Emotional Brain: The Mysterious Underpinnings of Emotional Life* (New York: Simon and Schuster, 1996); Leslie A. Brothers, *Friday's Footprint: How Society Shapes the Human Mind* (New York: Oxford University Press, 1997).

26. Terence Deacon and Ursula Goodenough, "The Sacred Emergence of Nature," in *The Oxford Handbook of Religion and Science*, ed. Philip Clayton (New York: Oxford University Press, 2008), 860.

27. Herbert H. Gintis, "Gene-Culture Coevolution and the Nature of Human Sociality," *Philosophical Transactions of the Royal Society, Biological Sciences* 2011 (366) 1566: 878–88.

28. See Rue, *Religion is Not about God*, 100.

29. For assorted contemporary debates, see Jane Maienschein and Michael Ruse, eds., *Biology and the Foundation of Ethics* (Cambridge: Cambridge University Press, 1999); Paul Lawrence Farber, *The Temptations of Evolutionary Ethics* (Berkeley and Los Angeles: University of California Press, 1998); Robert Wright, *The Moral Animal: Why We Are the Way We Are: The New Science of Evolutionary Psychology* (New York: Vintage, 1995); Richard Dawkins, *The Selfish Gene* (Oxford; New York: Oxford University Press, 1989); Edward O. Wilson, *On Human Nature* (Cambridge: Harvard University Press, 1988) and *Sociobiology: The New Synthesis* (Cambridge: Belknap Press of Harvard University Press, 2000); Gabriel Dover, *Dear Mr. Darwin: Letters on the Evolution of Life and Human Nature* (Berkeley and Los Angeles: University of California Press, 2000).

30. Konstantin Kolenda, *Religion without God* (Buffalo, N.Y.: Prometheus Books, 1976). Kolenda rejects the life-death dialectic that has become an influential conception of human reality for many Westerners. In this sense, his perspective is not unlike that of Heidegger, Camus, Sartre, and other major twentieth-century existential figures, whose philosophical and phenomenological reasoning offers important and serious appraisals of death. I build on his ideas in this chapter.

31. Ibid., 21.

32. Ibid.

33. Ibid., 26.

34. Ibid., 26–27.

35. There are many forms of consciousness, such as those associated with seeing, thinking, emotion, pain, and so on. Self-consciousness—that is, the self-referential aspect of consciousness—is probably a special case of consciousness.

36. David Chalmers, "Facing Up to the Problem of Consciousness," *The Journal of Consciousness Studies* 2, no. 3 (1995): 200.

37. Ibid., 201.

38. John R. Searle, *The Rediscovery of the Mind* (Cambridge, Mass.: MIT Press, 1994), 95.

39. Kolenda, *Religion without God*, 30.

40. Ibid., 42.

41. Shawn Copeland, *Enfleshing Freedom: Body, Race, and Being* (New York: Fortress Press, 2009).

42. William Shakespeare, *The Tempest*, ed. Burton Raffel (New Haven, Conn.: Yale University Press, 2006), 125.

43. Anna Julia Cooper, *A Voice from the South* (New York: Oxford University Press, 1988), 118.

44. W. E. B. Du Bois, *The Souls of Black Folk*, ed. Henry Louis Gates, Jr. and Terri Hume Oliver, A Norton & Company Critical Edition (New York: W. W. Norton, 1999).

45. James Baldwin, *The Cross of Redemption: Uncollected Writings* (New York: Vintage, 2010); *Baldwin: Collected Essays* (New York: Library of America, 1998).

3. ANNA JULIA COOPER: RELATIONAL HUMANITY
AND THE INTERPLAY OF ONE AND ALL

1. Cooper was born a slave in North Carolina on August 10, 1858, and later became an educator and social activist who firmly advocated educational rights for black women in North America. Her achievements as an intellectual and pioneering feminist are remarkable for the nineteenth century, especially when set against the backdrop of exploitation and degradation of black women in North America that was established with the systematic practice of involuntary servitude. For further study of her life and legacy, see Vivian M. May, *Anna Julia Cooper, Visionary Black Feminist* (New York: Routledge, 2007); Stephanie Y. Evans, "African American Women Scholars and International Research: Dr. Anna Julia Cooper's Legacy of Study Abroad," *Frontiers: The Interdisciplinary Journal of Study Abroad* 23 (2007): 77–100; Charles Lemert and Esme Bhan, eds., *The Voice of Anna Julia Cooper, Including "A Voice from the South" and Other Important Essays, Papers, and Letters* (Lanham, Md.: Rowman and Littlefield, 1998); Beverly Guy-Sheftall, "Black Feminist Studies: The Case of Anna Julia Cooper," *African American Review* 43, no.1 (Spring 2009): 11–15; Karen Baker-Fletcher, *A Singing Something: Womanist Reflections on Anna Julia Cooper* (New York: Crossroad, 1994); Shirley Moody-Turner, "Preface: Anna Julia Cooper: A Voice Beyond the South," *African American Review* 43, no. 1 (Spring 2009): 6–9; Kevin K. Gaines, *Uplifting the Race: Black Leadership, Politics, and Culture in the Twentieth Century* (Chapel Hill: University of North Carolina Press, 1996); Karen Johnson, *Uplifting the Women and the Race: The Lives, Educational Philosophies, and Social Activism of Anna Julia Cooper and Nannie Helen Burroughs*, Studies in African American History and Culture (New York: Routledge, 2000).

2. This chapter is an adapted version of my essay on Anna Julia Cooper published as "One and All: Anna Julia Cooper's Feminist Romanticism and

the Vision of Truth and Goodness" in the special issue on Anna Julia Cooper, ed. Ronald Sundstrom and Kathryn T. Gines, *Philosophia Africana* 12, no. 1 (March 2009): 83–106.

3 Anna Julia Cooper, *A Voice from the South* (New York: Oxford University Press, 1988), i. Further references to this work appear parenthetically in the main text.

4. Some feminist scholars have written on the political and social implications of Cooper's notion of voice, especially its purported representational aims—a gesture that some see as problematic and as evident of Cooper's class bias in speaking for poor black women of the South. See note 9 below.

5. In this discussion, I borrow from and am indebted to Saundra Morris's work on the figure of the Sphinx in Emerson's poetry and prose. For further readings, see Saundra Morris, "The Threshold Poem, Emerson, and 'The Sphinx,'" *American Literature* 69, no. 3 (September 1997): 547–70; "'Metre-Making' Arguments: Emerson's Poems," in *The Cambridge Companion to Ralph Waldo Emerson*, ed. Joel Porte and Saundra Morris (Cambridge: Cambridge University Press, 1999), 218–42; and "Through a Thousand Voices: Emerson's Poetry and 'The Sphinx,'" in *Emerson's Prose and Poetry*, ed. Joel Porte and Saundra Morris, Norton Critical Edition (New York: Norton, 2001), 777–90.

6. Morris, "Through a Thousand Voices," 777–90.

7. For further reading developing similar ideas, see Alfred N. Whitehead, *The Function of Reason* (Princeton: Princeton University Press, 1929) and *Process and Reality*, corrected ed., David Ray Griffin and Donald W. Sherburne, eds. (New York: Free Press, 1978).

8. Germaine Necker, otherwise known as Madame de Staël, was an important thinker and writer of the French Revolutionary and Napoleonic era, a woman around whom philosophers and politicians gathered. Mme de Staël's *Delphine* (1802) and *Corinne* (1807) were among the early examples of the Romantic style of writing.

9. See Mary Helen Washington, "Introduction," in Cooper, *Voice from the South*, xlvi; Baker-Fletcher, *A Singing Something*, 214.

10. Cooper seems to be defining *genius* as a type of natural capacity that can be developed and advanced with the proper nurturing. Cooper's usage of the term may be associated with her desire to establish a direct connection between the natural order of things and black vitality, creativity, and power. The modern meaning of genius has been associated with: 1) a natural ability or capacity; quality of mind; the special endowments that fit an individual for her peculiar work; 2) a native intellectual power that is attributed to those who are esteemed greatest in any arena of art, speculation, or practice; instinctive and extraordinary capacity for imaginative creation,

original thought, invention, or discovery. Genius in this second sense was often contrasted with talent. For further discussion of the complex lineage and variegated usage of the term *genius* among influential writers and artists in Western civilization, see Raymond Williams, *Keywords: A Vocabulary of Culture and Society* (New York: Oxford University Press, 1983), 143–44.

11. This section of ch. 3 is a condensed version of my discussion of the European Romantics' approach to nature found in the chapter on vitalism in my book *The Legacy of Anne Conway: Reverberations of a Mystical Naturalism* (Albany, N.Y.: SUNY Press), 2009.

12. See, for example, William Blake, "May God us keep / From Single Vision and Newton's sleep," in a letter of November 22, 1802 to T. Butts, in *Poetry and Prose of William Blake*, ed. Geoffrey Keynes (New York: Random House, 1927), 1068.

13. Robert Richards, *The Romantic Conception of Life: Science and Philosophy in the Age of Goethe* (Chicago: University of Chicago Press, 2002), 453–57. Goethe's aesthetic approach to nature, which was organic rather than geometrical, evolving rather than created, and based on sensibility and intuition rather than on imposed order, culminated in a "living quality" in which the subject and object are dissolved together in a poise of inquiry. He embraced neither teleological nor deterministic views of growth within every organism. Even as he emphasized the functional value of knowledge, Goethe also advanced a view of it that presupposes much more. For further reading, see R. H. Stephenson, *Goethe's Conception of Knowledge and Science* (Edinburgh: Edinburgh University Press, 1995).

14. Johann Wolfgang von Goethe, "Epirrhema," in *Goethe: The Collected Works*, vol. 1, *Selected Poems*, ed. Christopher Middleton (Princeton: Princeton University Press, 1994), 159.

15. See Ralph Waldo Emerson, "The Over-Soul," in *Essays and Lectures*, ed. Joel Porte (New York: Library of America, 1983), and Edward Haviland Miller, *Walt Whitman's "Song of Myself": A Mosaic of Interpretations* (Iowa City: University of Iowa Press, 1989). In the opening refrain of "Song of Myself," Whitman writes, "I CELEBRATE myself, and sing myself / And what I assume you shall assume / For every atom belonging to me as good belongs to you."

16. Transcendentalist authors who translated Goethe into English include Margaret Fuller, who translated *Torquato Tasso* (1834, 1860) and James Freeman Clarke, responsible for "Orphic Sayings from Goethe" (1836).

17. For an extended discussion, see Gustaaf Van Cromphout, *Emerson's Modernity and the Example of Goethe* (Columbia, Mo.: University of Missouri Press), 1990.

18. Emerson, "Over-Soul," 386.

19. See May, *Anna Julia Cooper*, 82.

20. Ibid., 53.

21. See Johann Wolfgang von Goethe, *The Metamorphosis of Plants* (Cambridge, Mass.; MIT Press, 2009), 5ff.

22. John Armstrong, *Love, Life, Goethe* (New York: Farrar, Straus and Giroux, 2006), 296. Armstrong notes that the seminal essay *The Metamorphosis of Plants* was written when Goethe was forty, weeks following the birth of his son, August, on Christmas Day, 1789.

23. According to Petra Rau, Johann Joachim Winckelmann associated *Bildung* with the classical-humanist knowledge of antiquity. In his 1795 counterrevolutionary treatise *Über die ästhetische Erziehung des Menschen* (*On the Aesthetic Education of Man*), Friedrich Schiller specifically included a political agenda in education and development. Furthermore, Wilhelm von Humboldt, who was influenced by a botanical and morphological framework from the natural sciences, achieved a grand synthetic and comprehensive definition of *Bildung* as a combination of *Anbildung* (acquisition of qualities or knowledge), *Ausbildung* (development of already existing qualities), *Entfaltung* (creative broadening of acquired skills or qualities without external restriction), and assimilation. For an extended discussion see Petra Rau, "Bildungsroman," *The Literary Encyclopedia*, vol. 1.4.1.01, *German-language Writing and Culture: Germany, 800–Present*, ed. Gerhard P. Knapp, Jennifer Marsten William, and Jill E. Twark, http://www.litencyc.com/php/stopics .php?rec=true&UID=119. Accessed 10 October 2015.

24. Armstrong, *Love, Life, Goethe*, 298.

25. Although Aristotle drew a distinction between matter and form, he also linked them through a distinct process of development. Matter, for Aristotle, contained the essential nature of all things, but only as a potential—the essence becomes real, or actual, via form. In other words, Aristotle posited matter as potency for form, where a thing's form is its essential or defining characteristics. The form of any inorganic or organic thing is its act, so that, for Aristotle, form is not inserted in some already existing body, but constitutes the body to be what it is from within itself. Thus, the natural world, as Aristotle conceived it, exhibits a collective dynamic that effects the transition from mere possibilities for a sector of nature to the realization of its full potential, its perfection (*entelecheia*). Although Aristotle's metaphysics was a type of substantialism, it was nonetheless pervasively processual and teleological— which may help to explain why these specific aspects of Aristotle's thought appear in Cooper's late-nineteenth-century feminist discourse.

26. Parts of this section are adapted from an earlier discussion found in my book *The Legacy of Anne Conway*, 82–84.

27. Henry Bergson, *Creative Evolution* (New York: Henry Holt, 1911), 47.

28. Whitehead, *Process and Reality*, 129; 161ff.

29. Ibid., 53.

30. Ibid., 59ff; 65–67; 76; 160ff.

31. Alfred N. Whitehead, *Adventures of Ideas* (New York: Free Press, 1933), 176ff.

32. Whitehead, *Process and Reality*, 23.

33. Whitehead, *Adventures of Ideas*, 226

34. Ibid., 99.

35. Whitehead, *Function of Reason*, 8.

4. W. E. B. DU BOIS: HUMANS AS CENTERS OF VALUE AND CREATIVITY

1. David Levering Lewis, *W. E. B. Du Bois: A Biography* (New York: Henry Holt, 2009), 26–27; hereafter cited as Lewis, *Biography*.

2. W. E. B. Du Bois, "Of Our Spiritual Strivings," *The Souls of Black Folk*, in *W. E. B. Du Bois: Writings* (New York: Library of America, 1986), 363–64; hereafter cited as Du Bois, *Souls*.

3. Ibid., 365.

4. Mary Keller, "On Re-cognizing W. E. B. Du Bois and Frantz Fanon in Two Volumes," in *Re-cognizing W. E. B. Du Bois in the Twenty-First Century: Essays on W. E. B. Du Bois*, ed. Mary Keller and Chester J. Fontenot, Jr. (Macon, Ga.: Mercer University Press, 2007), 3.

5. W. E. B. Du Bois, "Apology," *Dusk of Dawn*, in *W. E. B. Du Bois: Writings* (New York: Library of America, 1986), 551.

6. In keeping with the specific focus of this study, my discussion of Du Bois's racialized discourse intersects directly with an aspect of his work—his complex religiosity—that has been neglected by most scholars. In this chapter and throughout the book, I explore Du Bois's contribution to an extended view of humanity grounded in the tenets of religious naturalism. For a broader treatment of racial issues associated with Du Bois's theories and writings, see Lawrie Balfour, *Democracy's Reconstruction: Thinking Politically with W. E. B. Du Bois* (New York: Oxford University Press, 2011); Kwame Anthony Appiah, *Lines of Descent: W. E. B. Du Bois and the Emergence of Identity*, W. E. B. Du Bois Lectures (Cambridge, Mass.: Harvard University Press, 2014) and *In My Father's House: Africa in the Philosophy of Culture* (New York: Oxford University Press, 1993); Paul C. Taylor, *Race: A Philosophical Introduction* (Cambridge: Polity, 2013); Robert Gooding-Williams, *In the Shadow of Du Bois: Afro-Modern Political Thought in America* (Cambridge, Mass.: Harvard University Press, 2011) and *Look, A Negro! Philosophical Essays on Race, Culture, and Politics* (New York: Routledge, 2005).

7. Phil Zuckerman, *Du Bois on Religion* (Lanham, Md.: Altamira Press, 2000), 5–7. Zuckerman notes that religious themes, metaphors, and ref-

erences to God and Jesus permeate the body of Du Bois's work. He also contends that Du Bois saw religion as a social construction and a human projection that encapsulates both the wonders and warts of humanity and has the potential to exemplify one, the other, or both.

8. Among Du Bois's major writings on religion are *The Philadelphia Negro* (1899), which presented the first social survey of black congregations in an urban setting, and *The Negro Church* (1903), which provided the first in-depth sociological study of African American religion. In "The Problem of Amusement" (1897), Du Bois questions the failure of the black church to fulfill parishioners' earthly needs, and in "Religion in the South" (1907), he provides a scathing critique of white racism cloaked under the guise of Christianity. Du Bois also shared many thoughts on religion in *The Souls of Black Folk* (1903). He addressed religious themes in various literary and poetic writings as well, for example in the poems "Credo" and "The Prayers of God" from *Darkwater: Voices from within the Veil* (1920), and in the short stories "Jesus Christ in Georgia" (1911) and "The Gospel According to Mary Brown" (1920), both published in *The Crisis*. Furthermore, in numerous essays, letters, and speeches, Du Bois would evoke the pious expressions of slave spirituals, employ the trope of the jeremiad, advance the language of sacrifice, and make use of many biblical images. For a recent study of Du Bois's critique of structured religion, see Barbara E. Savage, "W. E. B. Du Bois and 'The Black Church,'" *Annals of the American Academy of Political and Social Sciences* 568, no. 1 (2000): 236.

9. W. E. B. Du Bois, *The Philadelphia Negro: A Social Study* (New York: Benjamin Blom, 1967), 21; quoted in Zuckerman, *Du Bois on Religion*, 9.

10. W. E. B. Du Bois, *John Brown*, ed. David R. Roediger (New York: Modern Library, 2001). Du Bois writes:

It is now *a full century* since this white-haired old man lay weltering in the blood which he spilled for broken and despised humanity. Let the nation which he loved and the South to which he spoke, reverently listen again today to those words, as prophetic now as then:

"You had better—all you people of the South—prepare yourselves for a settlement of this question. It must come up for settlement sooner than you are prepared for it, and the sooner you commence that preparation, the better for you. You may dispose of me very easily—I am nearly disposed of now; but this question is still to be settled—this Negro question, I mean. The end of that is not yet." (237)

11. Du Bois to Joseph B. Glenn, March 24, 1925, in *The World of W. E. B. Du Bois: A Quotation Sourcebook*, ed. Meyer Weinberg (Westport, Conn.:

Greenwood Press, 1992), 170. Cited hereafter as Weinberg, *Du Bois: Quotation Sourcebook*.

12. W. E. B. Du Bois, *Against Racism: Unpublished Essays, Papers, Addresses, 1887–1961*, ed. Herbert Aptheker (Amherst: University of Massachusetts Press, 1985), 84.

13. Du Bois, "Of Our Spiritual Strivings," *Souls*, 366.

14. W. E. B. Du Bois, *The Autobiography of W. E. B. Du Bois: A Soliloquy on Viewing My Life from the Last Decade of Its First Century* (New York: International Publishers, 1968), 285; hereafter cited as Du Bois, *Soliloquy*.

15. Lewis, *Biography*, 190.

16. Ibid., 191.

17. W. E. B. Du Bois, *Du Bois Speaks: Speeches and Addresses, 1920–1963*, ed. Philip S. Foner (New York, Pathfinder, 1970), 111.

18. Jonathon S. Kahn, *The Divine Discontent: The Religious Imagination of W. E. B. Du Bois* (New York: Oxford University Press, 2009).

19. W. E. B. Du Bois, "The Future of Wilberforce University," *Journal of Negro Education* 9, no. 4 (October 1940): 564–65; cited in Kahn, *Divine Discontent*, 3–4.

20. Kahn, *Divine Discontent*, 12.

21. Ibid., 8.

22. Ibid.

23. Jonathon S. Kahn, "The Pragmatic Religious Naturalism of W. E. B. Du Bois," in *The Souls of W. E. B. Du Bois: New Essays and Reflections*, ed. Edward J. Blum and Jason R. Young (Macon, Ga.: Macon University Press, 2009), 50–51.

24. Du Bois to Virginia Shattuck, 15 April 1937, in Weinberg, *Du Bois: Quotation Sourcebook*, 165.

25. W. E. B. Du Bois, "Immortality," in *W. E. B. Du Bois: A Reader*, ed. David Levering Lewis (New York: Holt, 1995), 134; hereafter cited as Lewis, *Reader*.

26. Ibid. See also Du Bois's admission in "De Senectute," a speech delivered at his eightieth birthday celebration: "It is quite possible that individual life does persist after death. If it does, I am not enthusiastic about it. I shall live it, of course, if I must, but not by choice. . . . I must prefer to do this one life reasonably well and stop." Quoted in Weinberg, *Du Bois: Quotation Sourcebook*, 166.

27. Du Bois to Larry and Carol Hautz, 29 September 1954, in Weinberg, *Du Bois: Quotation Sourcebook*, 170.

28. Du Bois, *Soliloquy*, 412.

29. Du Bois to A. P. Holly, April 7, 1925, in Weinberg, *Du Bois: Quotation Sourcebook*, 162.

30. Du Bois, *Soliloquy*, 43.

31. Du Bois to E. Pino Moreno, November 15, 1948, in *The Correspondence of W. E. B. Du Bois*, vol. 3, *Selections, 1944–1963*, ed. Herbert Aptheker (Amherst: University of Massachusetts Press, 1978), 223; hereafter cited as Aptheker, *Correspondence 3*.

32. Dwight Hopkins, "W. E. B. Du Bois on God and Jesus," in Blum and Young, *Souls of Du Bois*, 28.

33. Ibid., 29.

34. Anthony Pinn, "Charting Du Bois's Souls: Thoughts on 'Veiled' Bodies and the Study of Black Religion," in Blum and Young, *Souls of Du Bois*, 71.

35. Du Bois to Herbert Aptheker, January 10, 1956, in Aptheker, *Correspondence 3*, 395–96.

36. Kahn, "Pragmatic Religious Naturalism," 52.

37. Du Bois, "Of Our Spiritual Strivings," *Souls*, 365. Further references to this essay appear parenthetically in the main text.

38. My theoretical convictions in establishing the value and dignity of black humanity are based in the tenets of religious naturalism, as they are upheld by current scientific theories. In acknowledging this preference, I am suggesting that blacks' achievement of their humanity is a positive and possible goal based on our shared basic evolutionary impetus with other human organisms. As such, my view can be distinguished from some of the questions of ontology raised by critical and political theorists associated with an emerging strand of thought called Afro-pessimism. Current veins often revolve around a major assumption in political and critical theory that my work does not assume to address: namely, that the notion of slavery did not end in 1865, and that the United States has not squarely addressed the issues of black captivity vis-à-vis the myriad forms of black resistance. For further reading, see Jared Sexton, "The Social Life of Social Death: On Afro-Pessimism and Black Optimism," In*Tensions: E-Journal*, no. 5 (Fall/Winter 2011): 1–47, http://www.yorku.ca/intent/issue5/articles/jaredsexton.php; Saidiya Hartman, *Scenes of Subjection: Terror, Slavery, and Self-Making in Nineteenth-Century America* (New York: Oxford University Press, 1997) and *Lose Your Mother: A Journey along the Atlantic Slave Route* (New York: Farrar, Straus and Giroux, 2007); Joy James, ed., *Imprisoned Intellectuals: America's Political Prisoners Write on Life, Liberation, and Rebellion* (Lanham, Md.: Rowman and Littlefield, 2003); David Marriott, *On Black Men* (New York: Columbia University Press, 2000); Hortense Spillers, *Black, White, and in Color: Essays on American Literature and Culture* (Chicago: University of Chicago Press, 2003); Lewis Gordon, *Bad Faith and Antiblack Racism* (Atlantic Highlands, N.J.: Humanities Press, 1995); Frank B. Wilderson, *Incognegro: A Memoir of Exile and Apartheid*

(Brooklyn: South End Press, 2008), and *Red, White, and Black: Cinema and the Structure of U.S. Antagonisms* (Durham, N.C.: Duke University Press, 2010).

39. Lewis, *Biography*, 26.

40. Lewis, *Reader*, 3.

41. Pinn, "Charting Du Bois's Souls," 75.

5. JAMES BALDWIN: RELIGION, RACE, AND THE LOVE OF HUMANITY

1. Elsewhere I address more fully Baldwin's queer identity, outlining the ways he illuminated the complicated intersections of queerness, blackness, and religious rhetoric. In so doing, I evoke Melvin Dixon's extended use of the notion of *lieux de memoire* (sites of memory) to augment the importance of Baldwin's work for inaugurating a black queer sensibility that challenges traditional race-centered discourses in African American critical writing. For further reading, see Melvin Dixon, "The Black Writer's Use of Memory," in *A Melvin Dixon Critical Reader*, ed. Justin A. Joyce and Dwight A. McBride (Jackson: University Press of Mississippi, 2006), 55–70; Michael L. Cobb, "Pulptic Publicity: James Baldwin and the Queer Uses of Religious Words," *Journal of Gay and Lesbian Studies* 7, no. 2 (2001): 285–312. For further reading on Baldwin and the intersections of race and sexuality, see also Fred Stanley and Louis H. Pratt, *Conversations with James Baldwin* (Jackson: University Press of Mississippi, 1989); James Baldwin, "Notes for a Hypothetical Novel," in *Nobody Knows My Name* (New York: Vintage, 1992) and "Here Be Dragons," in *The Price of the Ticket: Collected Non-Fiction, 1948–1985* (New York: St. Martin's/Marek, 1985), 677–90; James Baldwin, James Mossman, and Colin MacInnes, "Race, Hate, Sex, and Colour: A Conversation," *Encounter* 25 (1965): 55–60; Magdalena Zaborowska, *James Baldwin's Turkish Decade: Erotics of Exile* (Durham, N.C.: Duke University Press, 2009).

2. In this book, I focus primarily on the interface of religion and race in Baldwin's writings, grounding his ideas in religious naturalism. In doing so, I seek to establish the epistemic groundings of a communal ontology in Baldwin's humanistic and racialized discourse. For further readings on Baldwin and race, specifically in fields such as political theory, see Jack Turner, *Awakening to Race: Individualism and Social Consciousness in America* (Chicago: University of Chicago Press, 2012). Turner has an interesting chapter on how Baldwin's racial views are amplified by a particular brand of individualism and self-reliance, which Turner distinguishes from traditional, popular views and also attributes to other iconic American figures. Another noteworthy study is Lawrie Balfour, *Evidence of Things Not Said: James Baldwin and the Promise of American Democracy* (Ithaca, N.Y.: Cornell University Press, 2000). Balfour positions Baldwin as a formidable contributor to democratic theory in light of contemporary debates about racial injustice.

3. Given the historical framework in which Baldwin was writing, his critiques target a problematic, limited binary constituted by the symbolic notions of whiteness and blackness. As current critical race theory suggests, however, racist discourse emerges from the dominance of a white supremacist ideology, or a master narrative that has failed to include the value and experiences of *all* groups whose identities have been isolated from and seen as distinct from "white" skin and everything associated with this distinction. In my own advancement of the sacred humanity concept, I wish to emphasize this broader notion of racialized discourse as having pertained to all marginalized voices and groups whose experiences have never been legitimized within this master narrative, even as I set the concept itself within the cultural and historical specificities of African Americans.

4. Cora Kaplan and Bill Schwartz, *James Baldwin: America and Beyond* (Ann Arbor: University of Michigan Press, 2011), 3.

5. James Baldwin, "Introduction to *Notes of a Native Son*, 1984," in *James Baldwin: Collected Essays* (New York: Library of America, 1998), 810. Hereafter, *James Baldwin: Collected Essays* is cited as *CE*.

6. Harold Bloom, "Introduction," in *James Baldwin: Modern Critical Views*, ed. Harold Bloom (New York: Chelsea House, 1986), 3. See also Melvin Dixon, *Ride Out the Wilderness: Geography and Identity in Afro-American Literature* (Urbana and Chicago: University of Illinois Press, 1987), 124.

7. Sondra A. O'Neale, "Fathers, Gods, and Religion: Perceptions of Christianity and Ethnic Faith in James Baldwin," in *Critical Essays on James Baldwin*, ed. Fred L. Standley and Nancy V. Burt (Boston: G. K. Hall, 1988), 140.

8. Douglas Field, "Pentecostalism and All That Jazz: Tracing James Baldwin's Religion," *Literature and Theology* 22, no. 4 (December 2008): 436–57.

9. Michael Lynch, "A Glimpse of the Hidden God: Dialectical Vision in Baldwin's *Go Tell it on the Mountain*," in *New Essays on "Go Tell it on the Mountain*," ed. Trudier Harris (Cambridge: Cambridge University Press, 1996), 32.

10. Field, "Pentecostalism and All That Jazz," 437.

11. Charles Hardy, *James Baldwin's God: Sex, Hope, and Crisis in Black Holiness Culture* (Knoxville: University of Tennessee Press, 2003).

12. Ibid., x.

13. "James Baldwin: About the Author," American Masters Series, PBS website, http://www.pbs.org/wnet/americanmasters/database/baldwin_j .html. Accessed September 2013.

14. Douglas Field, *All Those Strangers: The Art and Lives of James Baldwin* (Oxford: Oxford University Press, 2015), 83.

15. James Baldwin, "To Crush a Serpent," in *The Cross of Redemption: Uncollected Writings*, ed. Randall Kenan (New York: Vintage, 2010), 200. Hereafter, *Cross of Redemption* is cited as *CRUW*.

16. Clifford Geertz, "Religion as a Cultural System," in *Anthropological Approaches to the Study of Religion*, ed. Michael P. Banton (New York: Praeger Press, 1966), 1–46.

17. Baldwin, *The Fire Next Time*, CE, 302.

18. Baldwin, "To Crush a Serpent," *CRUW*, 196.

19. Baldwin, *The Fire Next Time*, CE, 304–5.

20. Ibid., 310.

21. Ibid., 309.

22. Ibid., 326.

23. Jean-Paul Sartre, *Existentialism and Human Emotions* (New York: Citadel Press/Kensington Publishing, 1987), 21–23.

24. Ibid., 29.

25. Baldwin, *Nobody Knows My Name*, CE, 137.

26. James Baldwin, "Stranger in a Swiss Village," in *Notes of a Native Son* (Boston: Beacon Press, 2012), 165.

27. Ibid., 172.

28. Baldwin, "The White Problem," *CRUW*, 90.

29. Ibid., 95.

30. Ibid., 89.

31. Baldwin, *The Fire Next Time*, CE, 339.

32. Baldwin, "The White Problem," *CRUW*, 90.

33. Baldwin, *The Fire Next Time*, CE, 309.

34. Sartre, *Existentialism and Human Emotions*, 52–59. Sartre's ontology defines two types of reality that lie beyond our conscious experience: the being of the object of consciousness and that of consciousness itself. The object of consciousness exists as "in-itself," that is, in an independent and nonrelational way. However, for Sartre, consciousness is always consciousness "of something," so it is defined in relation to something else, and it is not possible to grasp it within a conscious experience: it exists as "for-itself." In simpler terms, the being of inanimate things, like rocks, Sartre calls being-in-itself (*être-en-soi*). Being-for-itself (*être-pour-soi*) comprises beings that have feelings, human beings.

35. Baldwin, *The Fire Next Time*, CE, 343.

36. Ibid.

37. Hardy, *James Baldwin's God*, 47.

38. Baldwin, "We Can Change the Country," *CRUW*, 60.

39. Ibid., 60–61.

40. Baldwin, *The Fire Next Time*, CE, 291.

41. James Baldwin and Nikki Giovanni, *A Dialogue* (Philadelphia: Lippincott, 1975), 88–89.

42. Baldwin, *The Fire Next Time*, CE, 292.

43. Ibid.

44. Ibid., 293.

45. Ibid.

46. Cited in Hardy, *James Baldwin's God*, 48; 124 n. 35.

47. Baldwin, "Nothing Personal," CE, 694–95.

48. Baldwin, "What Price Freedom?" *CRUW*, 85.

49. Baldwin, "Of the Sorrow Songs: The Cross of Redemption," *CRUW*, 152.

50. Baldwin, *The Fire Next Time*, CE, 293–94.

51. Fred Standley and Louis H. Pratt, eds., *Conversations with James Baldwin* (Jackson: University Press of Mississippi, 1989), 50. See also Hardy, *James Baldwin's God*, 100–101, and Will Walker, "After *The Fire Next Time*: James Baldwin's Postconsensus Double Bind," in *Is It Nation Time? Contemporary Essays in Black Power and Black Nationalism*, ed. Eddie S. Glaude (Chicago: University of Chicago Press, 2002), 229.

52. Hardy, *James Baldwin's God*, 105. See also Cornel West, *Prophesy Deliverance! An Afro-American Revolutionary Christianity* (Philadelphia: Westminster Press, 1982).

53. Baldwin, "Autobiographical Notes," CE, 7.

54. Ibid., 8.

55. Baldwin, "Introduction to *Notes of a Native Son*, 1984," CE, 810.

56. Baldwin, *No Name in the Street*, CE, 468.

57. Baldwin, *The Fire Next Time*, CE, 334.

58. Ibid., 341.

59. James Baldwin, James Mossman, and Colin MacInnes, "Race, Hate, Sex, and Colour: A Conversation," *Encounter* 25 (1965): 55–60.

60. Baldwin, "To Crush a Serpent," *CRUW*, 203.

61. Baldwin, "Notes for a Hypothetical Novel: An Address," CE, 230.

62. D. Quentin Miller, ed., *Re-viewing James Baldwin: Things Not Seen* (Philadelphia: Temple University Press, 2000), 3.

63. Baldwin, *The Fire Next Time*, CE, 294.

CONCLUSION: TOWARD AN AFRICAN AMERICAN RELIGIOUS NATURALISM

1. Alfred N. Whitehead, *Science and the Modern World* (New York: Free Press, 1997), 191–92.

2. Peter H. Van Ness, *Spirituality and the Secular Quest* (New York: Crossroad, 1996), 5.

3. Donald Crosby, *Living with Ambiguity: Religious Naturalism and the Menace of Evil* (Albany: SUNY, 2008), ix–x.

4. Loyal Rue, *Religion Is Not about God: How Spiritual Traditions Nurture Our Biological Nature and What to Do When They Fail* (Piscataway, N.J.: Rutgers University Press, 2005), 77.

5. Ofelia Schutte, "Cultural Alterity: Cross-Cultural Communication and Feminist Theory in North-South Contexts," Border Crossings: Multicultural and Postcolonial Feminist Challenges to Philosophy, part 1, *Hypatia* 13, no. 2 (Spring 1998): 53–72.

6. Crosby, *Living with Ambiguity*, 5.

7. Stuart Kaufmann, *Reinventing the Sacred: A New View of Science, Reason, and Religion* (New York: Basic Books, 2010), xi.

8. Ibid, 6.

9. Wendell Berry, *Life Is a Miracle: An Essay against Modern Superstition* (Berkeley: Counterpoint, 2000), 13.

10. Ibid., 14.

11. Rue, *Religion Is Not about God*, 367.

12. Edward Said, "Orientalism Reconsidered," in *Literature, Politics, and Theory*, ed. Francis Barker et al. (London and New York: Methuen, 1986), 226.

13. Peter McFaren and Colin Lankshear, *Critical Literacy: Politics, Praxis, and the Postmodern* (Albany: SUNY Press, 1993), 42.

14. W. E. B. Du Bois, *The Autobiography: A Soliloquy on Viewing My Life from the Last Decade of Its First Century* (New York: International Publishers Press, 1968), 155.